THE ADVENT OF WAR 1939–40

Also by Roy Douglas

LAW FOR TECHNOLOGISTS
THE HISTORY OF THE LIBERAL PARTY 1895–1970
LAND, PEOPLE AND POLITICS: The land question in the
United Kingdom 1878–1952
IN THE YEAR OF MUNICH

THE ADVENT OF WAR
1939–40

Roy Douglas

Senior Lecturer, General Studies
University of Surrey

ST. MARTIN'S PRESS   NEW YORK

Library of Congress Cataloging in Publication Data

Douglas, Roy, 1924-
    The advent of war, 1939-40.

    Bibliography: p.
    Includes index.
    1. World War, 1939-1945. I. Title.
D755.1.D68   1979   940.53   78-12266
ISBN 0-312-00650-0

Contents

List of Plates

Preface

By the spring of 1939, most thinking people in Britain had probably decided that a major European war, involving their own country, was likely to arise in the next year or so. There were some aspects of that war which they doubtless guessed: that the allies on one side would include Britain, France and Poland; that the powers ranged against them would eventually include Germany and Italy. Yet there are many features of the early phases of that conflict which few people anticipated. Who imagined that the prelude to war would be an agreement between Germany and the Soviet Union – countries which were generally regarded on all sides as implacable enemies? Who thought that the first winter of war would see practically no fighting on land which involved Britain, Germany, France or Poland – but instead a great struggle between Russia and Finland? Who anticipated that, after six months of war, Italy, Romania and Yugoslavia would still be, technically, at peace? Who could have guessed the roles which Churchill or Lloyd George or Stalin would play?

In the last few years, many documents have become available for study, which make the events and personalities appear in an unfamiliar light. If we are to attempt a new look at the period in the light of evidence which was not available to historians a decade or so ago, then it is wise to exclude from our minds the interpretations which seemed reasonable enough to contemporaries who, by the nature of things, could not possibly have known all the facts. When – to take but one example – the British Government 'guaranteed' Poland at the end of March 1939, some apparently well-informed critics were astonished that the guarantee had been issued at that time, and in that manner. Why did the British Government not delay a few weeks, until it could announce that a great eastern alliance had been formed, incorporating not only Poland but also the Soviet Union and Romania? Why did that eastern alliance never come into being? Innumerable explanations have been given, which set varying shares of blame on Britain, France, Poland and the Soviet Union; but until the primary documents became available, conclusions were largely conjectural, and doubtless much influenced by the political bias of the commentators.

It is true that a large number of papers from the period were printed a few years after the war in the monumental *Documents on British Foreign Policy*. These documents, however, are only a selection – the tip of an iceberg. A great many diplomatic papers were not then available for inspection. Some were in private collections, to which the editors of the series did not have access. Other papers the editors may well have decided to exclude for other reasons: they contained, for example, possible libels on people still living; or the material was dangerous from the aspect of current diplomacy. Some very important papers are still sealed today; but at least it now seems that the great bulk of British material which has survived is currently available for study.

Much that was said or written about events shortly after they occurred made little pretence at objectivity. It was designed to guide behaviour in the future, rather than to provide a balanced record of the past. An element of polemics or apology persisted in many accounts which were written long afterwards. Some were composed by men who participated in the events and who – naturally enough – sought to defend their own actions; others by people who sought to derive a current political moral. Churchill, Attlee and Eden – to name but three – all wrote their own records of the period. All were major figures at the outbreak of war, and all were still at the centre of politics far into the 1950s. Even after the principal actors of the pre-war period had retired, men who had been closely associated with them still remained active in politics – and there was reason to think that the wisdom or unwisdom of principals might have rubbed off on juniors. Today, however, the great majority of men who played any significant part in events about the time of the outbreak of war are either dead or have retired from active politics. There is little political mileage to be made now by any review of 1939–40, however radical. That statement was not true fifteen – perhaps not ten – years ago.

The present author has concentrated on information which was available to British people at the time. Not all individuals had access to the same information, and if we wish to understand how they behaved it is well to remember that fact. When people in Britain needed to consider the aspirations, motives and policies of foreign countries – even of Allied countries – they could never do much more than make inspired guesses.

Before we praise or blame, we should try to understand. In order to do that, it is perhaps useful to start from the presumption that the measure of wisdom or unwisdom, of altruism or selfishness, or of most other moral properties, did not vary very greatly among the British individuals and groups which come under study. What did differ very greatly was their factual information, their past experiences and prejudices, and their current preoccupation.

Acknowledgements

I wish to express my gratitude to people who have helped in the production of this book. First I would like to thank those who have read part or all of the manuscript, and whose criticism has been absolutely invaluable; my wife; and Professor Otto Pick and Dr Teresa Poole of the University of Surrey. Thanks are also due to the librarians of several institutions, who have not only granted me access to archive material but have also often given me considerable help in using it to the best advantage: the University of Birmingham; London School of Economics; Churchill College, Cambridge; University College, Oxford; the National Maritime Museum; the Labour Party; the National Liberal Club; the Public Record Office; the Ulster Record Office; the National Library of Scotland. Permission is also gratefully acknowledged to the following for the use of copyright material: the University of Birmingham; University College, Oxford; Churchill College, Cambridge; the British Library of Political and Economic Science; the Labour Party; Viscount Caldecote; Lord Hankey; Earl Halifax; Lord Butler; Her Majesty's Stationery Office; the Beaverbrook Library. If any copyright owners have inadvertently been omitted, I apologise unreservedly. I would also like to express my appreciation to Lord Hailsham of St Marylebone for some helpful correspondence which has enabled me to appreciate much more accurately the rôle of the first Viscount Hailsham. Finally, I would like to thank the University of Surrey for grants from its Research Funds.

Readers of the book will note that I have not followed the practice of adhering strictly to the spellings used in original documents. Many personal and place names were commonly spelt in two or three different ways, and I felt that strict use of original orthography here would not really advance the cause of historical accuracy, but rather would produce confusion and irritation in the mind of the reader. As a general rule I have tried to spell names in the way preferred by the compatriots of an individual, or the residents in a locality.

ROY DOUGLAS

University of Surrey
February 1978

Scandinavia and the Baltic 1939–40

Central Europe, February 1939

1 The Die is Cast

'I can never forget that the ultimate decision, the Yes or No which
may decide the fate not only of all this generation but of the British
Empire itself, rests with me . . .' Neville to Hilda Chamberlain, 2
April 1939. NC 18/1/1092

When Neville Chamberlain became Prime Minister in May 1937,
there were already signs of serious deterioration in the international
situation. Many Britons had agonised over the Japanese attack on
China in 1931, or the Italian invasion of Abyssinia in 1935. Yet
these were remote events, which might stir anger, though scarcely
fear. The inception of the Spanish Civil War in 1936, and the active
intervention of other countries in the conflict, came closer to home;
but even on the Spanish question, where the wrath and apprehensions of political sophisticates were profoundly agitated, the public
at large was almost indifferent. 'Our own people,' wrote Hugh
Dalton, the Labour Party's chief spokesman on Foreign Affairs,
'were passionately concerned about Spain, but the great mass of the
people were not'.[1]

The foreign policy which the new Prime Minister inherited from
Stanley Baldwin centred on what was then called 'Appeasement'.
That word possesses several meanings, and the Prime Minister's
objective might be described today by another ambiguous term
'détente'. Chamberlain pressed this policy with a good deal more
positive determination than his empirical predecessor. He perceived that forces were at work which would necessarily lead to
great international changes in the near future, whatever he or others
might try to do. His objective was to help bring about those changes
without war.

It was the events of 1938 and the early months of 1939 which
really stirred both the statesmen and the British people as a whole.
When historic Vienna capitulated without a blow in March 1938,
the note of alarm was struck. Six months later, when it became
apparent that Hitler would risk war against Britain, France and

Russia combined in order to gain his ends in Czechoslovakia, then the menace was real beyond doubt.

Until the end of 1938, it was still possible to believe that 'Appeasement' had a chance of working. No doubt any deals which might be concluded with Hitler or Mussolini would have many objectionable features; but – provided the dictators were prepared to adhere to the arrangements they had made – such deals were infinitely preferable to war.

The event which finally caused the British Government to abandon appeasement in favour of armed resistance to Germany was the dismemberment of Czechoslovakia in March 1939. The process was complicated and messy.[2] The Germans compelled Slovakia to declare its 'independence'. Ruthenia, in the far east, was thus cut off from the Czech lands, and was promptly invaded by Hungary. The Czech President Hacha and Foreign Minister Chvalkovský were then summoned to Berlin, browbeaten in Hitler's well-known manner, and compelled to accede to the annexation of what remained of their country as a Protectorate of the German Reich.

On the afternoon of the annexation, Chamberlain told the House of Commons what he knew. Some of his information, though given in good faith, was later shown to be wrong. The occasion was charged with much acrimony, but everybody accepted that there was nothing Britain could do to help the Czechs.

As soon as men had time to think calmly about the matter, several sombre facts emerged. In the first place, it was now evident that Hitler's eastward designs had no discernible limit. When he seized Austria, when he annexed the Sudetenland, there was some argument for the view that he was merely bringing people of German speech and culture within the Reich. There was no shred of doubt, however, that the population of Bohemia and Moravia was overwhelmingly Czech, and thoroughly deplored the annexation. If the Czech lands could be taken in that way, what country in Europe was secure? In the second place, Hitler's very clear assurances over Czechoslovakia, given at the time of Munich, were manifestly worthless. Of course, he had broken other German undertakings long before. These, his apologists could argue, had been originally forced upon a weak, defeated, disarmed Germany. Not so the Munich agreement, concluded by the Führer himself on behalf of a strong Germany, less than six months earlier. The clear message to the world was that it was not possible to compound with

Nazi Germany, even on the most adverse terms; for any agreement which Hitler concluded would be violated the moment it suited his purpose. 'Appeasement', *détente*, call it what we will, was dead.

Other conclusions, no less baleful, might be drawn from the situation. Why did Hitler bother to annex Bohemia and Moravia? In September 1938 he had spoken of Czechoslovakia as 'a spear at his flank'. Whether such a spear ever existed is dubious in the extreme; but it manifestly did not exist at the beginning of 1939. The army was being rapidly disbanded. The country was completely at Germany's mercy, both militarily and economically. Why, then, should Hitler gratuitously offend and alert people in other countries who hitherto had proved amenable to his wishes? No doubt he sought to plunder Czechoslovakia's gold and currency reserves, but the quantity available seemed scarcely to justify the exercise. No; the only possible explanations seemed to be that the annexation had been undertaken with the object of seizing large stores of military material, or as a strategic base for attacks on other countries. Either explanation implied that Germany had much larger designs of future aggression. Such designs, it was now clear beyond doubt, could only be restrained by war or by threat of war.

Yet – one might ask – what was all this to Britain? A memorandum compiled by the Foreign Office for the Chiefs of Staff a fortnight after the seizure of Prague, demonstrates what might be called 'official thinking' on the matter:

> The absorption of Czecho-Slovakia has clearly revealed Germany's intention . . . there is every reason to suppose that the treatment applied in Czecho-Slovakia will be extended to other countries in Europe, notably Romania and Poland.[3]

Once this had been achieved, the authors of the document went on to add, 'the way will have been prepared for an attack on the west'.

Nobody in the Government was in a mood to confute this analysis. During the 'Appeasement' period, one alternative policy had been offered with great insistence by the Government's critics: rebel Conservatives like Winston Churchill, and the official spokesmen of the two Opposition Parties. It was a policy whose attraction had also been felt by some members of the Government. This policy involved some kind of 'Grand Alliance'. It was urged that all those countries which were immediately menaced by Germany, or were likely to be menaced in the near future, should join together in some kind of common declaration that any further act of German aggression would immediately involve them all in war with Germany. It was commonly assumed, (though seldom strictly argued), that a clear lead by Britain in that direction would be generally followed by the threatened states. If Germany can be stopped without war, so the argument ran, this is the only way to stop her. If she cannot be stopped without war, then the sooner that war is fought the greater the prospects of victory and the less the suffering which will be entailed. As soon as it became clear that 'Appeasement' had failed, the Government turned, with scarcely a thought for other possibilities, to the policy of the 'Grand Alliance'.

The fortnight which followed the German seizure of Prague was charged with the most alarming rumours from many different quarters. One set of reports suggested that Hungary and Romania were on the point of going to war. Another story told of large numbers of German troops on the Hungarian frontier. If this were true, was their intent to help Hungary in some common design against Romania, or to attack Hungary? At another point came news of twenty German divisions massing in the West, which seemed to suggest an imminent attack on France. The possibility that Germany might suddenly launch an air attack on London was taken quite seriously by the British Government, which ordered the army to man searchlights and anti-aircraft guns. The overwhelming impression which the historian receives from documents of the time – Cabinet papers, Foreign Office papers, and the Prime Minister's personal letters – is that the British Government had no means of deciding which reports were true and which false; while few people in diplomatic circles would have been astonished if war had broken out before the end of March. If Germany sought to spread confusion, she was certainly succeeding.

Some of the rumours were destined to become the cause, or at least the occasion, of very important and far-reaching decisions. On Saturday 18 March, the Cabinet was hastily summoned, in extraordinary circumstances. The Romanian Minister in London reported that his country had received a virtual ultimatum to submit to economic domination by Germany. The Romanian Foreign Minister denied the story but the representative in London persisted in his assertion. It required no deep military knowledge to see that Britain and France could not possibly intervene effectively to prevent Romania being overrun if Germany in alliance with Hungary decided to attack. The Cabinet approved

approaches to Russia, Poland, Yugoslavia, Turkey, Greece and
Romania with a view to obtaining assurances from them that
they would join with us in resisting any act of German aggression
aimed at obtaining domination in south-east Europe.[4]

A small sub-committee of senior Ministers was set up to draft the
appropriate telegrams. The Romanian 'ultimatum' which had
drawn the Cabinet together was apparently a considerable exag-
geration, and rather slipped from people's minds thereafter.

Away from Cabinet, however, the Ministers had second
thoughts. Was Poland in 'south-east Europe'? It was somewhat
monstrous to ask the Poles to join in defence of Romania, without
giving them corresponding assurances for their own country. There
were deeper and perhaps more intractable problems. Much delay
would be entailed if many states were to be brought into the
arrangements; while it was likely that the small states would 'adopt
a very rigid line about minor matters'.[5] It was better, decided the
sub-committee, to confine attention for the time being to the three
most important Powers: France, Russia and Poland. Furthermore,
a German move could occur in so many different directions and
ways that it was exceedingly difficult to devise an international
instrument which would provide against them all. The sub-
committee therefore decided that it would be wiser to take the 'not
very heroic' line of suggesting that the four Powers should agree on
'consultation' in the event of German aggression; the idea being that
action would probably follow the 'consultation'. The Cabinet was
therefore recalled on 20 March, and concurred in the new
proposals. Telegrams were written, and the drafts shown to
Cambon, Minister at the French Embassy in London. He declared
in favour of somewhat more emphatic documents, and this
remonstrance was accepted. At last the telegrams were despatched.
France returned a swift acceptance – as everyone had anticipated;
but neither Poland nor Russia was disposed to give a wholly
satisfactory reply.

While matters were still in these very preliminary stages, some
new pieces of information appeared. There were signs that both
Poland and Russia would fight if Romania were attacked. Germany
thereupon stole a march in a different direction, issuing peremptory
orders to Lithuania to cede the port of Memel. The population was
undoubtedly German, and the town had been occupied by the
Lithuanians a few years after the war in circumstances which were

widely deplored at the time. It was hardly possible to take a firm line over Memel.

The annexation of Memel highlighted another long-standing German complaint, rooted in the 1919 settlement. In order to give the new Poland access to the sea, the 'Polish Corridor' had been cut through an area of mixed Polish and German population, reaching the sea at Gdynia. East Prussia was thus severed from the bulk of Germany. Gdynia could not yet serve as a major port, and so the town of Danzig was created a 'Free City' under the League of Nations, with internal autonomy, but linked economically to Poland. The current population of Danzig, which stood at about 400,000, was overwhelmingly German.

The British proposal for a Four-Power Declaration more or less crossed with Russian proposals for a Six-Power Conference of threatened states, to be held at the Romanian capital of Bucharest. This was open to the same objections as the original British idea: the difficulty of securing any agreement between so many states with disparate interests. Russia, however, soon indicated that she was willing to support the original British plan; but only on condition that Poland would do the same. The Poles meanwhile showed their strongest apprehensions about any kind of association which included Russia – for reasons which we shall later have cause to consider.

By 27 March, the Cabinet Committee on Foreign Policy realised that there was no real chance of bringing Poland and Russia together into the sort of association that the Cabinet had originally envisaged. The Committee obviously regretted the Polish attitude, and various devices were discussed by which the Western Allies might become simultaneously linked to Russia and Poland, so that the effect of a four-Power association could be achieved indirectly. Nobody could feel great confidence in the likely success of such arrangements, and Britain might have to choose either Poland or Russia to the exclusion of the other. Whatever one thought of the relative military strengths of the two countries, there was the overriding fact that Poland bordered on Germany and Russia did not. This geographical consideration may have influenced the judgement of the Foreign Secretary, Viscount Halifax: 'that Poland would give the greater value'.[6] There were perceptible shades of opinion among the Ministers. Sir Samuel Hoare, currently Home Secretary, but a former Foreign Secretary himself, expressed strong regret at the exclusion of Russia, which 'would be regarded in many quarters as a considerable defeat for our policy'. Finally, however, the Foreign Policy Committee accepted the Prime Minister's proposal: to 'ascertain whether . . . if Poland or Romania are attacked directly or indirectly by Germany . . . they are prepared to resist. If so Great Britain and France would be prepared to support them'. This certainly did not mean that the idea of somehow effecting an association with Russia was to be abandoned. There was no doubt from the discussion that several important Ministers would continue to press strongly for such approaches.

The Prime Minister made it his business to discuss the proposal to guarantee Poland with the Parliamentary Opposition. Clement Attlee, Leader of the Labour Party, was indisposed, but the matter was raised with his deputy, Arthur Greenwood, who 'agreed that it was of the utmost importance to obtain the support of Poland and that it was impossible to secure that if Russia was brought into the declaration'.[7] To this observation, however, the Prime Minister was compelled to add a rider, when the matter was later reported to Cabinet:

Certain other members of the Opposition were . . . less amenable to this argument and it was likely that opposition would be raised to the Government's action from this point of view.[8]

The Cabinet meeting at which the new situation came under review was held on 29 March, two days after that of the Foreign Policy Committee. By this time there were persistent rumours that Germany had made proposals to Poland which included items like changes in the status of Danzig; construction of a motor road across the Corridor to link the two parts of Germany; and some kind of military arrangement between the two countries. It was by no means clear whether these proposals were peremptory, or what positive inducements had been offered. The official Polish view was that they had been communicated merely as *desiderata*.[9] Whatever the nature of the German approaches, it was tacitly assumed that the Poles should be discouraged from accepting them, and the Cabinet showed signs of moving towards the idea of some kind of unilateral assurance to Poland and possibly Romania; though the form which such assurances should take was far from certain.

Later in the same day, an extraordinary interview took place, which drove the Government to crystallise these somewhat vague proposals with considerable rapidity. The Berlin correspondent of a London newspaper met Chamberlain, Halifax and Sir Alexander Cadogan – Permanent Under-Secretary at the Foreign Office. The journalist adduced a considerable amount of evidence which indicated that Hitler proposed to follow his Memel coup with demands on Poland,

> which he proposed to split between annexation and protectorate. This would be followed by the absorption of Lithuania and then other states would be an easy prey. After that would come the possibility of a Russo-German alliance and finally the British Empire, the ultimate goal, would fall helplessly into the German maw.[10]

This was consistent with the current rumours about Poland; and some further oblique confirmation was received from observers. The Prime Minister feared that the German move would take place very suddenly and very soon: 'that we might wake up on Sunday or Monday morning to find Poland surrendering to an ultimatum'. Nobody with knowledge of Polish history or traditions would have entertained that particular fear; but few people in Britain knew much of Poland. If Chamberlain's view was correct, immediate action was essential to deter the Poles from surrender. The Cabinet was summoned for the following day.

It was agreed in Cabinet that a guarantee should be issued to Poland and announced the following day. Almost immediately after the meeting, evidence arrived which showed that no immediate German attack was likely;[11] but this did not deter anybody from proceeding with the agreed plan. The same evening Chamberlain met three leading members of the Labour Opposition, who 'told him that he would never get away with it tomorrow unless he brought in the Russians'.[12] The Prime Minister assured them that 'the absence of any reference to Russia in the declaration was based on expediency and not on any ideological consideration' – adding a pointed reference to 'the danger of alienating Poland at the present juncture'.[13]

The Labour members, whose concern with Russia was perhaps based on ideological rather than military considerations, were evidently reassured. When the announcement of the guarantee to Poland was made in the Commons the following day, the threatened explosion did not materialise. In the fuller debate a few days later the official spokesmen of Labour and the Liberals were disposed to welcome the announcement as a formal repudiation of Appeasement, and the first instalment of a new policy based on 'Collective Security' or 'Grand Alliance'. Not the least important speech came from Winston Churchill, so long a bitter critic of the foreign policy of the Government, who declared himself in 'almost complete agreement' with the line which was now being taken.

Yet there were others who evinced hesitation about any guarantee to Poland which was not supported by a clear agreement with Russia. Viscount Runciman was Lord President of the Council, but happened to be out of the country at the time of the Cabinet decision. He wrote with some anxiety to the Prime Minister:

> If Poland is not going all out in defence of her own country I cannot see why we should take on an unsupported cause. These telegrams suggest that Poland refuses to be associated with Soviet Russia. Doesn't this mean that we are going to be expected to come to the aid of a weaker alliance in order to please Poland?[14]

One must surmise that Runciman was satisfied with the explanations received on his return. Lord Hankey, who had retired a few months earlier from the post of Secretary to the Cabinet, expressed similar concern – judging (wrongly, as it happened) that these apprehensions had not been properly ventilated in Cabinet: 'The whole point is that *we* cannot save these eastern nations . . . We shall look terribly silly if [the Polish Foreign Minister] refuses to play with us and sillier still if Hitler goes in and knocks Poland out and we fail to help.'[15] Here Hankey was being thoroughly consistent; for he had deplored the French alliances with Poland and Czechoslovakia nearly a decade and a half earlier, on similar grounds.

More embarrassing to the Government was the criticism made in Parliament by Lloyd George, whose prestige as Prime Minister in the concluding stages of the First World War was still massive, and who had been a conspicuous advocate of Collective Security:

> If we are going in without help from Russia we are walking into a trap. It is the only country whose armies can get there . . . Unless the Poles are prepared to accept the only conditions with which we can successfully help them the responsibility must be theirs.

Lloyd George had long felt much sympathy with Russia and

noticeably less with Poland, and this no doubt influenced his comments. The authority of his name and the apparent validity of his arguments ensured serious attention; but whatever qualms some people felt in private, the pleasure of most Opposition critics when they learnt that the Government was 'standing up to Hitler' seems to have overborne these fears.

The Poles reacted to the 'guarantees' by 'sticking their toes in' to the German counter-proposals, and – according to the Italian Ambassador in Berlin – 'a violent anti-German feeling was being roused in Poland'.[16] Why, we may ask, were they prepared to make such a bold stand, particularly in view of their attitude to Russia? One British diplomat thought that the Poles calculated that they could hold Germany for a couple of months, at the end of which time the Nazi regime would collapse from within.[17] Perhaps they hoped for one of those miracles which have been plentiful in Polish history; while, on the other side, all experience suggested that any concessions would soon lead to destruction of their country's independence. Poland's stand was not only an act of egregious courage; perhaps there was a sort of desperate prudence there as well.

Early in April, Colonel Beck, Polish Foreign Minister and probably the most powerful man in his country, visited London for discussions.[18] Britain sought to broaden the arrangements so that it would be possible to include Russia, but met with steadfast refusal. Beck explained his country's attitude. The Poles were convinced that their national independence turned on maintaining a balance between Germany and Russia. If they leaned towards the latter, the former was likely to attack them. In the opinion of the Polish General Staff – corroborated by such information as Britain possessed – the Red Army might well prove efficient in defence of the Soviet Union, but would be of little value in offensive operations. Thus she could not give much positive help to Poland, but a Soviet alliance would do immense indirect damage. Another even deeper Polish fear was not much pressed by Beck on this occasion, but was constantly referred to in later talks with the Poles. They had every historical reason for fearing that if Russians once entered their country, they would prove exceedingly difficult to remove thereafter.

Several other important questions were discussed with Beck. Both Britain and Poland had mutual assistance treaties with France; if Germany attacked either party to the treaty, the other would go to

her aid. The Poles were willing to replace the recent British
guarantee by a similar bilateral Anglo-Polish treaty. During the
substantial period which would necessarily elapse before the
instrument was ready for ratification the arrangements on which
they had agreed would apply.[19] Several important matters were
raised, but not immediately cleared up: notably whether (on one
side) the treaty would be activated in the event of a German attack
on the Low Countries, and (on the other side) Britain would be
bound to come in if it was the Russians who attacked Poland. Both
points were resolved later to Britain's satisfaction; Poland undertook to fight in the event of a German assault on the Low Countries;
while a secret protocol to the eventual Treaty limited Britain's
obligations to the case of a German attack.[20]

Another matter discussed at the meetings with Beck threw diffuse
light on several current problems. If Germany could not immediately work her will on Poland, she was likely to turn to
Romania. Indeed, some members of the British Cabinet currently
believed that Romania was the principal danger spot.[21] Poland and
Romania already had a mutual assistance treaty against possible
Russian aggression; could they now broaden it to meet the common
danger from Germany? On the face of it, this seemed an eminently
sensible arrangement. Unfortunately there were complications.
Germany had no common frontier with Romania, and any attack
would be likely to involve collusion with Hungary. After the War,
Romania had acquired Transylvania from Hungary – a transfer
most bitterly resented, since the area contained many Magyars.
Thus far there had been a 'special relationship' between Poland and
Hungary; and through that relationship the Poles had perhaps
deterred Hungary from an attack on Romania a few weeks earlier.
If Poland allied with Romania against a possible invasion from the
west, this would be seen in Hungary as a ratification of the *status quo*
in Transylvania, and would utterly destroy her considerable moral
authority at Budapest. Thus it was wiser to leave matters as they
stood.

With Britain's attention centred on possible German aggression,
Italy took occasion on 7 April – Good Friday – to seize Albania. The
Powers had long recognised a kind of Italian suzerainty over
Albania, and the British Cabinet was clear that no action could be
taken to retrieve the situation: indeed, there was no serious proposal
from the Government's critics that there should be intervention.
Furthermore, there were some odd and ambiguous aspects to the

Italian move. There was no evidence to suggest that Mussolini had consulted with Hitler, beyond informing him at a late stage of the Italian intention. Albania itself was of little economic value. Did Italy make the move as part of wider designs in the Mediterranean; or in order to forestall Germany in relation to Yugoslavia? Perhaps neither plan was clearly conceived; in Halifax's view the Duce merely sought a cheap victory in order to prove to his compatriots that Germany was not the only country capable of seizing somebody else's territory.[22] Chamberlain at any rate was profoundly depressed by the Italian move, and took it as a personal affront: 'It cannot be denied that Mussolini has behaved to me like a sneak and a cad.'[23]

The Albanian incident served as a sharp reminder that Italy could not be ignored in diplomatic calculations, and deflected some attention from Germany to the Mediterranean. Fears were recorded – groundlessly, as it turned out – about a possible attack by Italy on the Greek island of Corfu.[24]

Attention soon returned to Romania – where, for once, it was the French who made the running. While Britain, with Italy in mind, was contemplating a guarantee to Greece, France indicated her intention to provide a similar guarantee to Romania. The British Cabinet was by no means convinced of the wisdom of such a guarantee – or that it could be honoured effectively in event of an attack. Lord Maugham, the Lord Chancellor, 'wondered whether it was necessary to give definite promises of assistance to such countries as Romania and Bulgaria and get nothing in return'.[25] If, however, the French made a declaration and Britain did not act with them, this would advertise to the world that serious differences existed between the Western Democracies. Halifax was convinced that the French proposal was unwise for other reasons, too; but there was no doubt about France's determination to guarantee Romania. In the event, a kind of compromise was achieved. The two Western countries issued simultaneous guarantees to Greece and Romania on 13 April.

In almost every respect, the problem of arranging a wide defensive bloc against German aggression was proving incomparably more difficult than had been envisaged by those who had talked glibly about a 'Grand Alliance' a year earlier. Practically every frontier in eastern Europe was resented by at least one of the bordering states – and some by both of them. Much had been said about Germany's grievances, and her intention to rectify those grievances by force. If Germany had been the only complainant, then an alliance against her might well have been feasible. Unfortunately the grievances felt by other countries were so great, and the corresponding fears experienced by their neighbours were so vivid, that it was scarcely necessary for Germany to play upon them in order to dissuade the other countries of Europe from collective resistance.

Yet practically everybody in British politics agreed that Germany should be confronted with a threat of war if any more important moves were made. People argued much about methods; very little about objectives. Lest any doubt should remain that the ill-feeling between Britain and Germany was reciprocal, Hitler made two announcements in his Reichstag speech on 29 April. The Anglo-German Naval Agreement of 1935 and 1937, which had limited Germany's fleet to 35 per cent of the British, was formally denounced. So also was the German-Polish Pact of 1934.

2 Reappraisals

'Conclusions. The situation is one in which the diplomatic authorities should consult with the military authorities.' Sir Redvers Buller to the 3rd Marquess of Salisbury, 5 September 1899. CAB 37/50/65

When we pass from a study of the diplomatic arrangements between Britain, France and Poland to an investigation of the military provisions which might underpin these arrangements, we move into a different world. We receive an eerie sense that the diplomats, and the politicians of all Parties, had been living in a world of fantasy.

The underlying theory of the new arrangements was – or rather had once been – logical enough. Let Germany be threatened with a war on two fronts if she committed aggression. Fear of that situation had been the besetting terror of German military planners since long before the 1914 war. With the 'two front' theory in mind, France had concluded alliances with Poland and Czechoslovakia in 1925. The new Anglo-Polish alliance was to be the keystone to the arch. Any war which Germany now waged must be fought on two fronts.

When we come to look at the military situation, such dreams vanish as in the light of day. In outline, the situation was well known not only to strategists, but to every reasonably well-informed layman. Germany had a very large, very well-equipped and highly mechanised army, supported by a formidable air force. France also had a very large and well-equipped army; but only a minuscule air force. She had, however, exceedingly strong eastern defences, the Maginot Line, which ran from the Alps to the Belgian frontier. The British navy was still the largest in the world. Only the United States and Japan had navies remotely approaching it; Germany was far behind. The British army was negligible; much smaller than it had been in 1914. The Royal Air Force was a good deal stronger than its French counterpart, but the two air forces together were far exceeded by that of Germany.

As for the third ally, Poland, no informed commentator had

much confidence in her capacity for prolonged resistance. At the Cabinet meeting which immediately preceded the British guarantee, Lord Chatfield – who by then had become Minister for Coordination of Defence – stated the military situation with engaging frankness: 'No doubt it would be impossible to prevent Poland being overrun. The Chiefs of Staff, indeed, thought that Poland would be likely to be overrun by Germany within two or three months.'[1] To put it rather crudely, Britain had 'guaranteed' Poland in full knowledge that she was thereby sending the Poles to their doom. There were many who thought that Russia might eventually rectify the situation to a degree; but even with Russian help there was not much prospect of saving Poland from eventual annihilation.

Was there a prospect of saving Poland, and also preserving the 'two-front war', in a different manner: by an Allied attack in the west, which would draw off enormous numbers of German troops from the east, and thus enable Poland to survive? In 1936, a representative of Poland had visited the Maginot Line. No doubt his hosts desired to impress him with their military might; but the view with which he returned to Poland was just the opposite of what had been intended. He was convinced that a country with such formidable defences would not voluntarily venture outside them. At the time of the 'Munich' crisis of September 1938, nobody in British official circles had been very sure whether France proposed a diversionary offensive in the west in the event of war over Czechoslovakia. General Gamelin, leader of the French armed forces, made a belated promise to launch an offensive in such circumstances; but nobody could feel confidence that it would be on a scale adequate to render any real assistance to the Czechs. Just before the guarantee to Poland there was similar uncertainty about French military intentions. It was admitted in Cabinet that no discussion had taken place with the French to ascertain whether they were prepared to make an attack on the Siegfried Line – Germany's western defences – to draw off troops from Poland.[2]

Thus, if the French themselves knew what they were going to do in event of war, they had apparently no intention of telling the British. Nor, we may add, had Britain much right to press them. If any offensive was launched in the west, it would be Frenchmen almost alone who would be participating. There was a further complication. On numerous occasions in the past few years, vital French secrets had leaked to the press or to the Germans, sometimes with catastrophic results. It is a fairly safe assumption that the

French General Staff would not say much to their own
Government – still less to the British. Thus politicians of both
countries were largely in the dark about the military position, and
had to conduct their diplomacy with very little real knowledge
about how the military situation was likely to develop if war came.

Nor was the Parliamentary Opposition in Britain in a position to
rectify the situation by timely criticism. In the serried ranks of the
Parliamentary Labour Party there was not one man who could lay
fair claim to being a real military expert. Critics like Lloyd George
and Churchill, whose views on military matters would have carried
real weight, were so obsessed with the essentially political
question of engineering a diplomatic alliance against Germany that
they could hardly devote equal attention to the military question of
how to wage war on Germany should need arise. Any close enquiry
into military plans and prospects would probably produce an effect
exactly the opposite of what the critics desired. People would see
with appalling clarity how grim the situation would be should war
come, and the new resolution which had appeared in the Western
Democracies would swiftly vanish.

Information which percolated through to the Government once
the Polish alliance was more or less an accomplished fact was by no
means reassuring. In the course of Anglo-French staff conversations
on 3 May 1939 – so the Cabinet was told three weeks later –

> there had been discussions as to what action should be taken if
> Germany stood strictly on the defensive in the west while
> attacking Poland in the east. According to the French repre-
> sentative, the intention of the French was that they would stand
> on the defensive on the Maginot Line, and would aim at building
> up a concentration which could take the offensive against Italy.
> But what would the position be if Italy were neutral? The French
> delegation had said that, if Belgium were in the war, the French
> would probably be prepared to undertake an offensive through
> that country, but that, if Belgium stayed out of the war, there was
> nothing to be done against the Siegfried Line.[3]

The French spokesman, admittedly, declared that he could not give
an authoritative statement of his country's position; but nothing
which happened later gave much reason for doubting the
statement's essential accuracy.

With such issues not finally resolved, some not unrelated domestic difficulties confronted the British Government. Most serious of these concerned the proposal to introduce compulsory military service. For many months there had existed a substantial movement in favour of conscription. The most ardent parliamentary spokesman was L. S. Amery and, among the press, the *Daily Express*. The Prime Minister had long accepted the view that it was inherently desirable, but did not consider it politically feasible. At the time of the crisis of September 1938, attention had been drawn to the fatuously small contribution which Britain would be able to make on land in event of war. There was not the slightest doubt that it would take years before she could field an army remotely comparable with that of France. The French began to raise increasingly broad hints that Britain – like most Continental nations – should adopt conscription. It gradually became evident that Britain's influence over France would largely turn on her ability to convince the French that she was prepared to make a significant military contribution. No doubt Britain's contribution by sea and in the air would be a good deal greater than that of France; but 'parity of sacrifice' – which the French demanded – meant risking a similar number of lives in battle.

Conscription, however, was fraught with considerable political difficulties. The Labour Party had tacitly accepted the need for rearmament, and the trade unions were co-operating considerably with the Government in that field. Yet the Labour Party was firmly opposed to conscription, and the strength of that opposition lay more with trade unionists who feared it would be used as a precedent for 'industrial conscription' than with the residue of pacifist opinion among 'socialist intellectuals'. Furthermore, Stanley Baldwin had made a famous promise in April 1936 that he would not introduce conscription so long as peace prevailed, and Chamberlain himself had renewed that undertaking.[4] The purely military argument was by no means 'open and shut'. If war came at all, it would surely come soon, and no measure of conscription which Britain could apply would significantly affect Germany's willingness to make war, or the early course of that war. The Government's majority was adequate to bulldoze any opposition; but if the trade unions proved really truculent, the damage which would follow would far more than balance any military advantage. Yet some members of the Cabinet, and particularly the Secretary for War, Leslie Hore-Belisha, had long been convinced that conscription was necessary.

The argument which eventually persuaded the Cabinet to grasp the bull by the horns was curiously oblique. In the latter part of March, Chamberlain feared a sudden air attack on London. Although that particular emergency was met, the Prime Minister resolved 'to see that our defences shall be manned day and night all the year round'.[5] On 19 April, the question of establishing permanent anti-aircraft defence was raised in Cabinet. Hore-Belisha informed his colleagues that 'he saw no means of obtaining the additional Regulars required for a permanent arrangement except by some system of compulsory service'.[6] Lord Chatfield was not impressed by the argument. To introduce military conscription to meet a contingency of that kind was 'employing a sledge-hammer to crack a nut'. Chamberlain and Halifax supported Hore-Belisha's proposal, but for different reasons; what seemed to concern them most was the need to satisfy France. The matter was remitted for later discussion.

The plan for Compulsory Military Training which was submitted by the War Office after this discussion was of limited scope.[7] It was not designed to introduce conscription permanently, but for a provisional period of three years. During that period, the scheme could be terminated by Order in Council; while it might be extended year by year thereafter if Parliament specifically assented. Men of a defined age-group – this was later fixed at twenty – would be called up for six months' service; thereafter, they would be required to undertake part-time Territorial training for a further three and a half years. The total number of men in the age-group was about 300,000; when the medically unfit had been excluded, this would yield about 200,000 to 250,000 – corresponding roughly with the War Office requirements. About 80,000 conscripts would be needed for home defence against air attack; the remainder would be included in special training units, or attached to units of the Regular Army. Voluntary recruitment for the Regular Army would continue; and conscripts would not be raised for the navy or the air force.

The War Office gave considerable attention to political aspects of the proposal. It was designed as a measure which,

> while it may not secure the active support of the labour movement, may at least avoid arousing their strong opposition. This is important, since the introduction of this measure will only constitute an effective demonstration of the spirit of this country,

if it is presented in a form which will secure a wide measure of approval.[8]

The scheme was discussed in Cabinet on 24 April. Chamberlain felt that the point of Baldwin's 1936 pledge could be met: 'while we were not actually at war, it was a mockery to call the present conditions "peace" and these undertakings did not therefore disturb him'.[9] In order to 'soften up' criticism further, the Prime Minister proposed to see leaders of the TUC and of the Labour Party before an announcement was made. On these terms, conscription was accepted by the Cabinet without difficulty.

In Parliament, criticism was somewhat perfunctory. 'The Labour Party', wrote Chamberlain to his sister, describing the debate,

> were divided in their opposition, and I could see that the back-benchers were shaken when I made my appeal to them. They listened to me in silence with serious faces . . . I am told that they may very possibly decide to take the line that having made their protest there is no object in pressing their opposition much further. This is very different from their first attitude when we were told that we were going to have 'hell with the lid off'.[10]

In the event, Labour did divide the House, and succeeded *inter alia* in dividing the Parliamentary Liberals almost mathematically between pro-Government, anti-Government and abstainers; but no serious campaign against conscription followed. According to Dalton,[11] 'a message was brought to [Labour's] Parliamentary Executive via an intermediary to Attlee and Greenwood that, in his view, if there were too vehement opposition to conscription, the chance of Hitler pulling the trigger would be increased by 25%'. The conscription Bill took a considerable time to pass into law, but this was due to the lethargy of Parliamentary procedure, not to the force of political opposition. When war eventually came, a structure had already been set up which enabled the Government gradually to extend the scope of conscription to meet requirements.

How much value this force ever was to the Allied cause is a matter of continuing debate. Something may be said for the view that the existence of pre-war conscription contributed considerably to the British loss at Dunkirk, without assisting the preservation of either France or Poland. What is quite evident, however, is that the primary object of conscription was neither to strengthen Britain militarily nor to deter Germany, but to increase British influence over France.

In what cause, we may ask, did Britain seek to exert that influence? Not to help Poland, or to prolong the two-front war by causing the French to do battle. Perhaps, to a minor extent, to give some more power to the British elbow when complaints were made (as repeatedly happened) about the weakness of the French air force and the slackness of French aircraft production. More than either of these things, the object was diplomatic. It was all too clear, even at this stage of the proceedings, that there existed a great bulk of opinion in France which viewed any prospect of war against Germany with alarm close to terror. Evidence that Britain was doing what lay in her power to raise a large army might go some way to persuade the French that Britain would involve herself fully in any war in which France was engaged. In one sense, Britain desired to stiffen French determination; yet, in another sense, she desired to hold France back from involving herself and Britain, too, in obligations which neither country could hope to fulfil: obligations whose purpose was not to restrain or to defeat Germany, but to draw some of the German fire away from France.

3 Russia: Stage One

'Diplomacy is the art of saying "Good doggie" while you are looking for a stick.' Anon.

In the early part of 1939, most critics of the Government treated one proposition as axiomatic. Germany and Russia were implacable enemies. Russia was therefore willing and anxious to join with the Western Democracies, Poland, and any other threatened state in common defence against Germany. If that common defence were not established, it would be the fault of one or more of the other Allies, who refused to give Russia proper consideration as a Great Power, or refused reasonable conditions required by the Soviet Union which were essential for an effective alliance. At the time of Munich – so the story ran – Russia had been cold-shouldered by Britain and France, with disastrous results. This must not happen again!

A not dissimilar view was widely taken in diplomatic, and even in government, circles. At the turn of the year a new Ambassador to Moscow, Sir William Seeds, was appointed. This appeared a good opportunity to review British policy towards the Soviet Union. Lord Halifax sought the view of his Chief Diplomatic Adviser at the Foreign Office, Sir Robert Vansittart, and received a forthright answer: 'Anglo-Russian relations are in a most unsatisfactory state. It is not only regrettable but dangerous that they should be in that state, and a continuance of it will become a great deal more dangerous very shortly.'[1] Vansittart argued that the Russians required a 'gesture', and suggested sending a Cabinet Minister to Russia. Halifax was interested in the idea, but it was not taken up; instead, R. S. Hudson, a junior Minister, was despatched on a Trade Mission to Moscow. Announcement of Hudson's mission was followed swiftly by the German seizure of Prague, and then by the discussions aimed at a Four-Power Declaration, or some other kind of close link between the various threatened states.

We have already seen something of the difficulties which Britain and France encountered when they attempted to erect a simple common front against German expansion. It was impossible to state bluntly in public the gravamen of Poland's difficulty. Opposition politicians – or the man-in-the-street – could be excused, on the evidence available to them, for thinking that either Poland was being unreasonably intransigent, or the Western Allies were not putting much effort into winning Russian assistance on reasonable terms. Some people believed even darker things about the British Government: that they wished to encourage Hitler to destroy Russia. There is no evidence to suggest that anyone of importance had any such wish at this time. Indeed, the facts of geography prescribed that Hitler could only attack Russia by passing through Poland; and nobody in Britain wanted him to do that.

Even senior members of the Government had been taken aback at the intensity of Polish feeling about Russia, as evidenced at the time of Beck's visit to London early in April. And Poland was not the only country to take this attitude. When the Romanian Foreign Secretary visited London a few weeks later, Lord Halifax admitted that he had been 'surprised at the strength of M. Gafencu's feelings about Russia'.[2] Events would later show that these Polish and Romanian fears were justified to the hilt; but it was immediately certain that any British Government which sought to organise an East European bloc to resist Germany must take full account of them.

Other countries shared those apprehensions. Diplomats began to talk about possible 'guarantees' and 'assistance' which might be given by Russia to her various neighbours. The words 'guarantee' and 'assistance' have a very different meaning in diplomatic parlance from the man-in-the-street's model of one man promising or rendering help to another who is set upon by a bully. The terms on which Russia proffered 'guarantees' and 'assistance' made them look uncommonly like threats. Maxim Litvinov, Soviet Commissar for Foreign Affairs, told the Latvian Minister in Moscow 'that any voluntary or forced alienation of Latvian independence would affect the Soviet Union, which could not remain a disinterested spectator'.[3] He spoke in similar terms to the Estonians. In other words, if those countries made unwelcome concessions to Germany – even if those concessions were made as part of some free and reciprocal arrangement – Russia proposed to intervene. Finland was in a somewhat stronger position, but her apprehensions were similar; the Finnish Foreign Minister declared that a Soviet 'guarantee' would be

> incompatible with the autonomy and sovereignty of Finland. The only attitude to take towards any state disposed, in virtue of the guarantee undertaken on its own initiative, to furnish its so-called assistance when it considers this to be required by the state which it claims to protect, is to regard such a measure as aggression.[4]

Thus every single European state bordering on the Soviet Union, from the Arctic Sea to the Black Sea, felt the gravest possible apprehensions about 'guarantees' or 'assistance' which Russia might offer, in the lively fear that these words would prove euphemisms for Soviet invasion. Their own country would become a battlefield between Russia and Germany, and would lose its precarious independence, whoever won. All of them had long experience of Russian rule over part or the whole of their country; and the memory of Russian troops – whether Tsarist or Bolshevik – had not been pleasant.

The British Government faced difficulties from another quarter: the self-governing Dominions. New Zealand was the only one which pressed unreservedly for 'Russian assistance in the prevention of aggression'.[5] Australia insisted that any agreement with Russia should not apply to the Far East, for 'we attach great importance to preserving friendship with Japan'.[6] Russia and Japan were regarded as inveterate enemies; Australia herself would be menaced if a Russian alliance turned Japan into an enemy. The South African Cabinet declared in April that 'bilateral obligations with Russia should if possible be avoided'; when negotiations had reached a more crucial stage a month later, they feared that adoption of the Russian proposals 'will close the door to peace and make war almost inevitable'.[7] Mackenzie King, Prime Minister of Canada, apparently associated himself with what he described as the 'considerable opposition in Canada to the manner in which the United Kingdom appears to be becoming entangled with the Balkan and Eastern European countries and above all with Russia'.[8]

Thus British statesmen had good cause to meditate on the price they would have to pay for an alliance with Russia, even if that alliance could be obtained at all. The risk of war might be substantially increased. The morality of Allied cause would be

sullied if they were forced to encompass Russian aggression in order
to counter German aggression, and sympathetic neutrals would be
alienated. Finally, links with the self-governing Dominions would
be strained to the limit. Not many people in Britain would have
been willing to forgo the sympathy and help of Canada and
Australia in order to achieve a dubious alliance with Russia.

For a moment, British diplomats thought that there was a
possible way of employing the Russian threat against German
expansion, without simultaneously stirring the lively fears of
Russia's western neighbours. Stalin had recently declared that the
Soviet Union stood for 'rendering all support to nations which are
victims of aggression and which fight for their independence'. On 14
April the Soviet Ambassador, Ivan Maisky, told Halifax that his
Government sought the British view 'as to the best method by which
[Russian] assistance could be given and as to the part the various
Powers could play in helping Romania'.[9] While this only referred
directly to one of the threatened countries, yet the problems of the
others were not dissimilar. The Foreign Secretary therefore instructed Seeds to suggest that Russia should make a declaration.

> that in event of any act of aggression against any European
> neighbour of the Soviet Union which was resisted by the country
> concerned, the assistance of the Soviet Government would be
> available, if desired, and would be afforded in such manner as
> would be found most convenient.[10]

The Russians, however, had very different ideas. A few days later,
Soviet counter-proposals were communicated to the British Ambassador. Britain, France and the Soviet Union should conclude a
long-term agreement for mutual assistance in event of a German
attack on any one of them, or on any state lying between the Baltic
and Black Seas. The Russian proposals included other collateral
suggestions: Britain, for example, should explain to Poland that the
recent guarantee was exclusively concerned with possible aggression from Germany.[11] Britain already had that point very much
in mind; she was well aware that she could not possibly render
Poland effective help against an attack from the only other possible
quarter; but Russia's concern on the matter was hardly reassuring.
The Ambassador to Warsaw commented rather mildly that 'Any
idea that such proposals had even been put forward would be liable
to jeopardise possibility of Polish-Soviet cooperation.'[12] The com-

ment of the British Foreign Office, communicated to the next meeting of the Cabinet's Foreign Policy Committee, opened with two very engaging and frank observations:

1. The Russian proposal is extremely inconvenient.
2. What it really comes to is that we have to balance the advantage of a paper commitment by Russia to join in a war on our side against the disadvantage of associating ourselves openly with Russia.[13]

Ministers had not lost hope of an arrangement with Russia on the lines of the British suggestion, but there was certainly some danger that Russia would only join the anti-German front on terms broadly similar to her own proposals: terms which would include – whatever else – a full-scale alliance with Britain and France, in which the Western Democracies would not be too fastidious about the territorial integrity of states lying between Germany and Russia. Apart from the moral and international difficulties which would be posed by such an arrangement, British statesmen – as we have seen – were disposed to doubt how valuable a Russian alliance would prove, from a purely military point of view.

Very little 'hard' information existed on this crucial question. Stalin's reign of terror ensured that Russians were exceedingly unwilling to maintain any contacts with Western diplomats, who thus could get no direct evidence about conditions prevailing in the Soviet Union, or the state of the country's armed forces after the massive purge of 1937. An appraisal by the Chiefs of Staff was urgently required, and was at last produced on 24 April.[14] In the first three months of war, they considered, Russia could mobilise on her western frontier 30 cavalry and 100 infantry divisions. The most impressive feature was some 9000 tanks 'of a high quality'. In other respects, however, the Chiefs of Staff felt that Russian equipment was 'more noteworthy for its quantity rather than for its quality'; and Chatfield added his own gloss for the Cabinet's Foreign Policy Committee. Of the theoretical 130 divisions, he considered that Russia 'would not in practice be able to maintain in the field on that frontier more than about thirty divisions'.[15]

The Chiefs of Staff thought that 'The Russian army in particular has suffered from the purge in 1937 and from the political control of the Commissar system. Its value, especially for offensive operations, has thus been much reduced.'[16] More serious still were the logistic problems of Russia rendering aid to Poland – even on the assumption that both countries were willing that such aid should be given:

> Communications are in a deplorable condition. There are five single and one double railway lines leading from Russia to Poland. Rolling stock and engines on those railways are poor, and we understand that from 30 to 60% are usually undergoing repair at the same time.

The Appreciation went on to mention the break of railway gauge at the Polish frontier; the absence of any organisation to receive and maintain Russian forces; the 'inadequate and indifferent' character of the roads; and the absence of sufficient mechanical transport. The Chiefs of Staff therefore decided 'that any substantial Russian military support to Poland is out of the question'. They went on to add that the possibilities of support to Romania were not much better.

More positively, the Chiefs of Staff felt that Russia could probably resist a German invasion of the Baltic States, and tie down substantial German forces on the eastern frontier. The Russian navy would be active both in the Baltic and in the Far East, where it would 'be an added deterrent to Japan from undertaking any large-scale operations against Australia, New Zealand or Singapore'. The Russian air force would be of some use against Germany in the west, and also in the east in containing Japan. Russian assistance would undeniably prove of some military value; but, as Chatfield observed, 'was not nearly as great as certain quarters represented it to be'.[17] However, what seems to have concerned the Chiefs of Staff most was the other side of the medal: the danger which nobody (and least of all Russia's admirers) cared to bruit in public: 'the very grave military dangers inherent in the possibility of any agreement between Germany and Russia'.[18] Perhaps the Chiefs of Staff had some inkling that German minds were already beginning to consider that possibility.

If Britain and Russia both found it impossible to accept each other's proposals, and yet both desired an alliance, were there any other possibilities? France also had received proposals from Russia, and the French had considered lines of a possible reply. It was clearly very important that the two Western Democracies should co-ordinate their answers.

The French view, and much of later French diplomacy in relation to Russia, must be seen in the context of France's military position. In event of war, France was obviously in more imminent danger of German invasion than Britain – or, for that matter, Russia. While all three countries at this stage may have desired that a strong eastern front should be organised against Germany, the construction of that front was a matter of far more urgent concern to France than to the others. Britain, from her position of comparative security, could – as it were – afford to feel scruples about the interests of Russia's Western neighbours. France could not. What appalled the French beyond measure was the prospect that they might find themselves facing the full might of an undivided German attack, without continuing support from eastern allies. While the French would doubtless have preferred the British proposals to the Russian, they were more interested that Britain and Russia should come to terms than in what those terms might be.

The French proposed that if any of the three Great Powers became engaged in war with Germany as a result of executing international engagements in Central or Eastern Europe, the others would assist; meanwhile, the three countries would consult urgently on the nature of that assistance.[19] These proposals did not appeal either to the Foreign Policy Committee or to the Cabinet. Even if Russia was prepared to accept them, they would be likely to produce hostile reactions in Warsaw and Bucharest, which would break the common front which Britain had been at such pains to establish.

Leaving aside the question of the merits of the French proposal, however, there was a rather serious diplomatic danger inherent in the situation. Britain was thinking on the lines of somehow modifying her original proposals to allay Russia's fear that she might find herself fighting alone. France was thinking on the lines of acceding, with some modifications, to Russia's proposal. The 'first essential', decided the Cabinet Foreign Policy Committee, was to ensure that France did not reply to Russia without communicating with Britain.[20] The British Government was therefore horrified to learn, on 3 May, that Foreign Minister Georges Bonnet had disclosed the French proposals to the Russian Ambassador in Paris.[21] Bonnet's assurance that this revelation had been made 'in the heat of the conversation and in order to dispel suspicions of Mr. Souritch' scarcely carried conviction, and would hardly have reflected well on Bonnet's capacity if it had been true.

The following day came further news, which may have been related to the French disclosure. Litvinov had been replaced by Molotov as Soviet Commissar for Foreign Affairs. As Seeds had met Litvinov very recently, and had received no inkling of the impending change,[22] this bore all appearance of a sudden decision by Stalin. Bland assurances were given that Soviet foreign policy was unchanged; but diplomats in Moscow regarded the move as a blow for the Western Powers, and Russian press attacks on Germany and Italy suddenly ceased.[23] More bad news swiftly followed. A Non-Aggression Pact was concluded between Germany and Latvia, and there was information that similar negotiations were proceeding between Germany and Estonia.[24] Worse still, on 8 May Germany and Italy announced that they were converting the Rome-Berlin Axis into a political and military pact.[25] Perhaps these matters, too, were indirectly related to the manifest difficulties of arranging some effective agreement between the Western Democracies and Russia.

In the afternoon of 8 May, Seeds had his first interview with the new Commissar for Foreign Affairs. The Ambassador had at last been instructed to deliver the British reply. Like the earlier British proposal, it recommended a unilateral Russian declaration; but this time suggested that Russia should make her participation in war contingent on Britain and France being also involved.

The interview proved exceedingly uncomfortable for Seeds. Molotov pointed out that the Soviet Union had made similar proposals to Britain and France, but received different replies. Did each of the Western Governments approve of the other's answer? The Commissar reminded the Ambassador of a recent Parliamentary statement by Sir John Simon, Chancellor of the Exchequer, to the effect that Britain was willing to conclude a military alliance with Russia. Was this an authoritative statement of the British view? Seeds, not having a full transcript of Simon's statement in front of him, could hardly reply. Finally, Molotov observed that the Soviet Union had replied to British proposals in three days; while Britain, by contrast, had taken three weeks to answer Russia.[26] It would not have added much to the prospects of an arrangement between Britain and Russia if the Ambassador had given the real answer – which, in any event, Molotov doubtless knew. The delay had been caused by the extreme difficulty in making any kind of statement which did not do violence to British opinion outside or even within the Government. Simon had spoken the complete truth when he said 'there is no objection on our part in principle' to a military alliance. The objection had lain elsewhere; and Britain – unlike France – was not prepared to give Russia *carte blanche* to invade neighbouring countries. Finally – Seeds might have added – it was easy for Russia to return an early reply, for a totalitarian state does not need to bother about placating internal criticism; and a country with no allies has no cause to worry about the susceptibilities of others.

Not only did Molotov give Seeds a most unpleasant interview, he also provided no answer to the current proposals – even though these were designed to remove all Russian fears that she might find herself fighting alone against German aggression. This time it took Russia rather longer to concoct a reply. The answer was given by Molotov to Seeds on 15 May. Several criticisms of the current British proposals were made: criticisms, one feels, which the British Government could fairly easily have met by amendments to those proposals. The most serious feature of the Soviet reply was a flat statement that Russia set 'at least three indispensable conditions' for any agreement:

(i) The conclusion between England[*sic*], France and the U.S.S.R. of an effective pact of mutual assistance against aggression,

(ii) The guarantee by those three Great Powers of states of Central and Eastern Europe threatened by aggression including also Latvia, Estonia and Finland,

(iii) The conclusion of a concrete agreement between England, France and U.S.S.R. as to forms and extent of assistance to be rendered materially to each other and to the guaranteed States.[27]

Thus it was no longer a question whether some compromise could be reached between the British and Russian ideas, but of whether Britain would concede the essentials which Russia was demanding, or whether the negotiations should fail.

France again pressed that her own terms formed an acceptable basis of agreement. By now even the placid Halifax was becoming a little testy, and told a French diplomat:

The Soviet Government had, in my opinion, been the reverse of helpful, and I hoped he would forgive me for saying that I thought their attitude might, in part, have been influenced by

M. Bonnet's action, of which he himself had told us . . . in giving the Soviet Ambassador the alternative draft proposed by the French Government that went very much further than our own.[28]

The British Government now needed to consider the military consequences which would follow if – on one hand – the Russian demand were accepted, or – on the other hand – the negotiations collapsed. The Chiefs of Staff sent an *aide-mémoire*, pointing out that failure to conclude agreement would not only be a diplomatic defeat, but would also have

serious military repercussions . . . encouraging Germany – ultimately throwing the U.S.S.R. into her arms. Even if this did not occur, we certainly want something better than the bare neutrality of Russia, not only from the point of view of being able to draw on her resources, but also to enable assistance to be rendered to Poland and Romania. Furthermore, if Russia remained neutral, it would leave her in a dominating position at the end of hostilities.[29]

The feature of the Soviet proposals which seems most to have disturbed the military advisers was the proposed guarantee to the Baltic States which – 'from a strictly military point of view' – Britain should refuse to give. They did not, however, take very seriously the danger of a German attack on Russia via the Baltic States, which did not also involve violation of Poland. Apparently Sir Robert Vansittart was able to impress even Maisky with the force of these arguments.[30]

The cabinet had insisted that a final decision which would involve acceptance or rejection of an agreement with Russia must be their own, and not that of the Foreign Policy Committee; but the latter body had two rather inconclusive meetings at which they discussed what lead they might give. Hoare, Chatfield, Stanley and Halifax were rather more keen on acceptance than were Chamberlain, Inskip or W. S. Morrison; but nobody declared flatly against acceptance.

It is useful to ask why Russia was proving so difficult. The Prime Minister was as mystified as anyone. 'I wish I know what sort of people we are dealing with,' he wrote to his sister,

They may be just simple straightforward people but I cannot rid myself of the suspicion that they are chiefly concerned to see the 'capitalist' powers tear each other to pieces while they stay out themselves . . .Those who advocate [making an alliance] say that if we don't agree Russia and Germany will come to an understanding, which to my mind is a pretty sinister commentary on Russian reliability. But some of the members of the Cabinet who were most unwilling to agree to the alliance now appear to have swung round to the opposite view.[31]

The difficulty encountered in concluding an arrangement between Britain and Russia thus seemed to admit of two very different explanations. According to one of these explanations, Russia's overwhelming concern was to see that somebody else did any fighting which might follow. According to the other explanation, the Russians were not sure that Britain was serious, and required to be convinced. Halifax was able to discuss the matter frankly with Maisky. The Russian Government, concluded the Foreign Secretary,

> were mainly concerned with the two following points: first, they were not prepared to be put in a position of inequality as compared with the British, French and Polish Governments, which had concluded agreements on a reciprocal basis; secondly, Russia feared that Romania and Poland might collapse and that if this happened, the condition which we made that these countries should resist German aggression would not fulfilled. Russia would thus be left face to face with Germany without any assurance of support from us.[32]

The triple relationship was a *sine qua non*: 'M. Maisky had said that if we were prepared to accept this fundamental condition, the Russians would not prove difficult on other matters.' In the report sent by Halifax to the Foreign Office, the Soviet position was discussed further. Maisky had argued that there were two possible courses of action for Russia. If the tripartite pact were concluded, then Germany would be contained without war. 'Even the present negotiations', he observed, 'had made [Hitler] proceed with caution, since he was not sure what would come out of them'.[33] The second possibility for Russia, argued Maisky, was that she should 'take care of herself and enter into no obligation to other Powers'. In that event, war was likely. Russia, thought the Soviet Ambassador, could win that war, but could not prevent it. Thus, from the Soviet point of view a tripartite pact was desirable.

On 24 May, Halifax argued strenuously in Cabinet for acceptance, in principle, of some kind of three-Power pact. There were indications, he suggested, that Poland and Romania might be reconciled to this arrangement, and the difficulties of the Baltic States overcome. Chamberlain, in spite of his 'considerable misgivings' about an alliance, argued for the same view. Breakdown of negotiations, felt the Prime Minister, would have a bad effect on public opinion in Europe, and would prove particularly discouraging to France and Turkey – especially so soon after the conclusion of a German-Italian Pact. In a private letter he added: 'There was no sign of opposition to the alliance in the press and it was obvious that refusal would create immense difficulties in the House even if I could persuade my Cabinet.'[34] It was Sir Samuel Hoare who provided the most hopeful suggestion: one which seemed to meet objections from all sides. Let the three Powers conclude what was in substance a tripartite pact, but in form a very different kind of arrangement. Let them announce that aggression against a European state which requested assistance from Britain and France would activate obligations on those Powers under Article XVI of the League of Nations. If Britain and France went to the victim's aid, the Soviet Union would follow, without awaiting a meeting of the League. Whatever reservations Chamberlain – or, for that matter, the Russians – might have regarding a long-term agreement, it certainly looked as if there was a good chance that an arrangement could be achieved on these lines. Poland's fear that Russia would invade without invitation would be removed; so also would Russia's fears that she might be left fighting alone. Hitler would be checked from attacking Poland, for he would realise that Poland had power to call down everyone else upon him. The suggestion was accepted with evident relief by the Cabinet.

The same afternoon, Chamberlain made a brief statement in Parliament

indicating that he had every reason to hope that as a result of proposals which His Majesty's Government are now in a position to make on main questions arising, it will be found possible to reach agreement at an early date, though there remain some further points to be cleared up.[35]

The French approved, and even Maisky 'said he thought agreement should now prove possible'.[36] If all Powers really meant what they had been saying, there seemed every hope that these unusually sanguine assertions would soon be realised.

4 Russia: Stage Two

'But I don't like a policy which leaves us to face any mess into which bankrupt France may be dragged by barbarian Russia.' Viscount Morley to the Earl of Rosebery, 7 August 1914. Rosebery papers, Box 37, National Library of Scotland

'The treacherous cynicism of Stalin & Co, with our military mission sitting and negotiating in Moscow is beyond belief . . . I wish that I thought that it would shock the blind faith of the Opposition in the Soviet virtues . . .' Sir Nevile Henderson to Viscount Halifax 22 August 1939. FO 800/316, fo. 217 seq.

In the afternoon of 27 May 1939 – three days after Chamberlain's encouraging announcement – Molotov summonded the Western diplomatic representatives at Moscow, and told them that his personal reaction to the new initiative of their Governments was negative.[1] On 2 June he followed this gloomy warning by a new draft – which, he suggested, was a modification of their own proposals, designed to meet the views of the Soviet Union. Two points in particular exercised the Russians. First, there should be 'concrete agreement as to the form and extent of assistance'. This question would later prove of great importance, but did not play a large part in discussions for several weeks. Much more immediate attention was given to Molotov's second point. The three Great Powers, he considered, should issue what were euphemistically called 'guarantees' to the Baltic States. This geographical term was coming to be used in a rather unusual way, to cover Estonia, Latvia and Finland. 'Clearly,' explained Halifax to the Foreign Policy Committee,

> the Soviet Government feared, or pretended to fear, that the three Baltic States might not, when subjected to German aggression, turn to Russia for help, and indeed might acquiesce more or less willingly in Germany's aggression. The result would be very serious so far as Russia was concerned.[2]

Russia therefore proposed that Britain and France should join with her in 'guaranteeing' Estonia, Latvia and Finland; while she would join with them in their existing guarantees to Belgium, Greece, Turkey, Romania and Poland. Thereafter, 'the three Great Powers should come to each other's help if one of them became involved in war . . . as a result of aggression . . . against any of the eight named States.'

The Foreign Policy Committee decided that the next step in proceedings should be to recall Seeds for consultation, to apprise him fully of the views of the British Government. A day or two later, however, the Ambassador developed influenza, and was unable to travel. It was therefore arranged that a senior Foreign Office official, William Strang, should go to Moscow to advise him on the conversations.[3] A great cry went up, both in Russia and in British Opposition quarters, to the effect that it was an insult to the Soviet Union to send a man who was not a major public figure. Chamberlain, with some irritation, pointed out the misunderstanding which underlay that criticism; Strang would function 'not as a Plenipotentiary but as an Expert Adviser to assist H. M. Ambassador in explaining the point of view of H. M. Government to the Soviet Ministers'.[4] The Prime Minister's private correspondence evinced his continuing deep mystification about Russia's reason for raising these various difficulties:

> I can't make up my mind whether the Bolshies are double-crossing us and trying to make difficulties or whether they are only showing the cunning and suspicion of the peasant. On the whole I incline to the latter view, but I am sure they are greatly encouraged by the Opposition and the Winston-Eden-Lloyd George group with whom Maisky is in constant touch.[5]

Anthony Eden approached Halifax and volunteered to go as an envoy to Moscow. The Foreign Secretary was at first receptive of this suggestion, but the Prime Minister dissuaded him. Chamberlain saw these moves as part of a design by these political critics to win entry to the Cabinet, and eventually perhaps replace him by 'a more amenable Prime Minister'.

Proteracted and weary discussions about the proposed Alliance continued. Various difficulties emerged, some more tractable than others. Russia pointed out that if the three Powers were to conclude a treaty which might involve them as allies in war, then each should undertake not to make a separate peace with Germany. The Foreign Policy Committee decided that if agreement could be reached on all other points, the United Kingdom should fall in with Russia's views on that one.[6] As Halifax put it rather dryly to the Cabinet, 'If, for example, the Russian Government sought to keep this country fighting for some fantastic object, common sense would, he thought, reassert itself.'[7]

More serious was the problem of the proposed guarantees. By 20 June, the Foreign Policy Committee learnt that Molotov was not prepared to conclude any agreement involving countries outside the three Great Powers unless Britain would join in guarantees to the Baltic States. If this proposal was unacceptable, the Soviet Commissar suggested a 'simple tripartite pact' between Britain, France and Russia, to operate in event of a direct German attack on any one of them. This suggestion horrified Oliver Stanley, President of the Board of Trade. In his view, 'Such an arrangement would generally be regarded as a complete breakdown of the negotiations and . . . it would be generally feared that Germany would seize Danzig, and that if war resulted Russia would not be involved.'[8] Others were less disturbed: the pro-Russian Sir Samuel Hoare considered that Molotov's new proposal, if brought into effect, 'would have a good effect on world opinion, and would be much less dangerous and embarrassing to us than the more elaborate arrangement'.

Reactions in the Baltic States themselves were violently hostile to the proposed guarantees. The Estonian Foreign Secretary declared that if

> a Great Power desired to assume the rôle of our defender either as representing the collective system or to defend its own vital interests in the Baltic, such a system would be considered an aggression against which the Baltic States are prepared to fight with all their forces.[9]

His Finnish counterpart, as we have seen, had already spoken in very similar language.[10] Nevertheless, the British Government was not anxious to abandon the idea of a full-scale alliance altogether. At last, on 26 June, a fairly clear point of view began to emerge from the Foreign Policy Committee. Britain would concur in guarantees to the Baltic States if Russia would join in similar guarantees to Switzerland and the Netherlands. If Russia would not reciprocate, then the general feeling seemed to be that it would be better to fall back on Molotov's 'simple tripartite pact'; but there was no emphatic decision on the matter.[11] Nor did the Cabinet, which met two days later, attempt to reach a final decision.[12]

Within a few days, it became clear that Russia would not participate in the reciprocal guarantees to Holland and Switzerland; but she continued to demand that the Western Democracies should guarantee the Baltic States as an essential condition for any arrangement broader than the suggested 'simple tripartite pact'. As Halifax observed ruefully, 'the wheel has thus come full circle from the early days of the negotiations, when Russia had pressed for full reciprocity'.[13] By contrast, Beck of Poland by then felt 'no objection to an Anglo-Soviet Pact though . . . he has warned the British not to expect too much by way of material aid from Russia, even if the pact is signed'.[14]

Not merely was Russia unwilling to afford reciprocity over the guarantees, but she now made a further demand. The guarantees, declared the Soviet Union, should apply not merely to direct aggression but to 'indirect aggression' as well. Russia proposed a definition of the latter term which included 'an internal *coup d'état* or a reversal of policy in the interests of the aggressor'. This would manifestly give Russia almost limitless power to intervene in the affairs of the 'guaranteed' states, and might compel the Western Democracies to go to war in support of such Russian intervention.

When the Foreign Policy Committee met on 4 July, Halifax argued that there were only two possibilities: to break off negotiations – 'this course he did not favour' – or to fall back on Molotov's own proposal for a simple tripartite pact. The pact might perhaps be strengthened by inserting provision for immediate consultations 'as to the methods, form and extent of assistance . . . and provisions for consultation in regard to cases not covered by the Pact'.[15] The Committee was not greatly disturbed about Russia's refusal to participate in guarantees to Switzerland and the Netherlands. As Sir Samuel Hoare pointed out, 'the war was unlikely to begin in either country'. The Committee was much more deeply divided over whether the 'simple tripartite pact' was an acceptable arrangement, since it would not cover the case of Danzig and the Corridor. The alternative was apparently capitulation to Russia's demands over 'indirect aggression'. At that Chamberlain baulked completely: 'He was convinced that it would be quite impossible for us to justify and defend in public acceptance of this definition which he regarded with the utmost apprehension.' Stanley put forward the

proposal which was eventually accepted. Britain should concede
the Russian demand to omit Holland and Switzerland, provided
the Soviet Union would drop the objectionable definition of
'indirect aggression'. If not, then it was better to fall back on the
'simple tripartite pact'. What, we may ask, of Stanley's point about
Danzig? Chamberlain replied that Hitler would probably assume
that the agreement contained secret provisions, and therefore
decide to avoid 'provocative action'. There were obvious risks in the
bluff on Hitler; but it appeared better than the alternative of letting
the world know that the talks had collapsed.

On the following day, the Cabinet accepted the Foreign Policy
Committee's proposals.[16] The matter was now apparently for
Russia to choose: either drop the definition of 'indirect aggression –
in which case Britain would cease to insist on the reciprocal
guarantees to Switzerland and the Netherlands; or else, if Russia
preferred, revert to Molotov's own proposal of a 'simple tripartite
pact'.

Instead of answering this apparently straightforward question,
the Russians returned to the point which Molotov had mentioned in
Moscow on 27 May, and which had been almost completely
omitted from discussions for a fortnight. The political agreement,
they declared, should not come into effect until the parties had
concluded a military agreement. Here a sharp divergence was
observed between Britain and France.[17] Britain disliked the
guarantees very much and the definition of 'indirect aggression'
even more; but had no serious objection to Russia's proposal of a
military agreement. France, at first, had no objection to Russia's
view on the first two questions, but strongly opposed the suggestion
that military conversations should be entered before political
agreement had been concluded. The French were fairly easily
brought round to the British view on the first pair of proposals, but
resisted the third with considerable determination. They eventually
not merely capitulated on that point, too, but (as we shall see) went
a great deal further, to the high embarrassment of the British.

Even the physical conditions in which the Moscow talks were
conducted were evidently designed to humiliate the British and
French:

M. Molotov sat aloft enthroned with the two Ambassadors on a
much lower level. M. Molotov constantly left the meeting, no
doubt to obtain information or guidance from higher authority,

and whenever the Ambassadors attempted to maintain a sustained argument, M. Molotov interrupted them by saying that the Soviet Government had given their decision and that they should pass to the next item on the Agenda.[18]

The Prime Minister gave his own bleak summary of the extent to which Russia was exerting herself to meet difficulties from the Western Powers: 'Up to the present time, no move in the direction of concessions great or small of any sort or kind has been made by the Soviet Government since the negotiations opened.'

At the Cabinet of 19 July, the once sanguine Halifax reported his own gloomy view: a 'simple tripartite pact' was 'the only alternative to a complete breakdown'. Even the former seemed unlikely – 'he was rather disposed to think that the Soviet Government were not very keen on concluding an agreement of any kind'. In that case, one might ask (although apparently nobody did), why should the Soviet Union bother to keep the negotiations going at all, and not take the first reasonable excuse for breaking them off? There was a hint of an answer at the Cabinet meeting, when Halifax reported 'that discussions of some kind were proceeding between the German Government and the Soviet Government'. While the Foreign Secretary declared that 'it was impossible to assess their real value', he guessed that they 'related to industrial matters'.[19]

The Foreign Policy Committee met immediately after the Cabinet. Interpreting the Cabinet discussions, they decided that Halifax should contact the French; but in any event Britain would not tolerate the Soviet definition of 'indirect aggression'. She would be prepared, if necessary, to concede the Soviet point that political and military agreements should be formally concluded at the same time; but only on the understanding that there should be no military conversations until political agreement had been reached.[20]

The French Foreign Minister reacted to this relatively firm British stand by sending an immediate personal message to Halifax – which may only be seen as an impassioned plea for concessions to just about anything the Russians might choose to demand. The French, who had hung back on the proposal for military conversations, were now far more eager to comply with Soviet wishes than were the British. If the negotiations failed, Bonnet declared,

'Il ne faut pas dissimuler l'éffet désastreux, non seulement pour

nos deux Pays, mais pour le maintien de la paix . . . Les
opinions publiques y attachent dans tous les pays la plus grande
importance. Elle a pris de ce fait même un caractère
symbolique . . .'[21]

The French collapse infuriated Chamberlain:

> With great difficulty I got my colleagues to agree with me taking
> a firm line with [the Russians] and then the French ran out. After
> talking very 'higgity' about the necessity for digging one's toes in,
> they suddenly collapsed and said that 'to save the peace' we must
> get an agreement 'at all costs'. I was thoroughly disgusted.[22]

The Prime Minister would not consider conceding the Russian view
on the 'guarantees' – 'a formula', he observed, 'which would drive
the Baltic States and Finland into Germany's arms'. On the other
hand, he was forced to yield to the French over the military
negotiations. The Foreign Policy Committee's decision was over-
ruled, and on 21 July Halifax sent new instructions to Seeds. The
Foreign Secretary was 'prepared in the last resort to agree to the
immediate initiation of military conversations without waiting for
final agreement' on the definition of 'indirect aggression' – adding:
'I do not like this and should only wish to advance this suggestion if
danger of breakdown . . . seems imminent.'[23]
On 23 July, Molotov and the Ambassadors again met. Little was
said about 'indirect aggression', but when news was given that the
Western Democracies had agreed that political and military
agreements should come into force simultaneously, 'this had given
great satisfaction to M. Molotov who had asked whether the
military conversations could start at once'.[24]
Halifax eagerly advised the Cabinet to accept this suggestion:

> It seemed likely that willingness to start military conversations
> was regarded by the Russians as a test of our good faith. He
> thought that the opening of these conversations would have a
> good effect on world opinion, although he did not disguise his
> view that the conversations would take a long time.

In the ensuing Cabinet discussion, at least one (unidentified)
Minister pointed out that this would involve giving confidential
information to the Soviet Government before any pact had been

concluded with them. However, 'there was a general agreement that our representatives should be instructed to proceed very slowly with the conversations until a political pact had been concluded'. On that salutary note of caution the matter was left, and arrangements were eventually made for the military mission to depart by merchant ship for Russia on 5 August.[25] The military conversations appeared to begin well. Then the Russians raised the question whether the Poles and Romanians would allow them to operate through their countries in event of war. The British and French delegates 'had suggested that the Russians should approach, Poland and Romania directly, but after withdrawing for an hour for consultation, the Soviet delegation, headed by Molotov, returned and . . . demanded that the British and French should act as intermediaries'.[26] 'Otherwise, in the Soviet Government's view, it would be useless to continue the conversations.'[27]

Poland was approached first. The Chief of the Polish General Staff gave the usual Polish answer. If the Russians were admitted into Poland, Germany would promptly attack. Further enquiries revealed another Polish apprehension which was being raised increasingly: 'that in their view the Russian objective was to find an excuse to occupy Polish territory permanently'. According to Count Raczynski, Polish Ambassador in London,

> The Russians demanded that they should have the right 'in order to make contact with the Germans' to take over the administration of two large areas of Poland, (1) the Vilna Corridor, to be administered from Vilna, and (2) East Galicia, to be administered from Lwow. This proposal had been rejected by the Poles on the ground that it was already a new partition of Poland. No plans, so far as he knew, had been made for the supply of materials and munitions by Russia to the Poles.[28]

Even in face of this, the Poles were not otherwise intransigent; the Polish Government 'would be prepared to consider a Memorandum regarding military cooperation with the Soviets, based on the Staff Conversations in Moscow'.[29]

At this point, French wishful thinking took command. 'An affirmative answer on the question of principle' was prepared by the French representative, although there appears some doubt whether that answer was ever actually delivered. Halifax was invited to return a similar answer to the Russians on Britain's behalf, 'but had not felt it right to do so'. More embarrassing still, the French thereupon instructed their military representatives to tell Russia that they authorised Soviet passage through Poland as soon as the latter was at war with Germany. Not long afterwards the talks collapsed, for reasons which soon became all too clear.

The discussions had served some purpose, though not the one which the Western Allies intended. Lord Chatfield confessed to the Cabinet: 'In the course of the Staff Conversations we had given the Soviet Government certain information as regards our plans on the Western Front, but only in general terms. The French had given a good deal more detailed information.'[30]

While the military conversations continued, Parliament was in recess. The Cabinet met on 2 August, and then dispersed for the summer, in the hope rather than anticipation that Ministers might enjoy a substantial period of recuperation from their labours. On 22 August, the Cabinet was suddenly convened in extraordinary circumstances. Von Ribbentrop, German Foreign Minister, was on his way to Moscow. Press reports – still not officially confirmed – told of an impending German-Soviet Non-Aggression Pact. If this were true, there was certainly no point in resuming the conversations with Russia, which had done enough damage already. The Prime Minister assured Greenwood that 'he had no prior information at all about the German-Russian Pact'.[31] There remained the theoretical possibility that Russia's object was merely to force the Western Powers to agree to her terms for a pact with them; but such a suggestion hardly carried conviction.

Next day, further light was cast on dark places. On 23 August, the Non-Aggression Pact was formally signed in Moscow between Molotov and Ribbentrop, with Stalin beaming beside them. To remove any conceivable doubts, Article 2 provided that if either Russia or Germany were engaged in war with a third Power, the other would in no way support that Power. Obviously Germany proposed to attack Poland very soon, and equally obviously Russia had received her price for allowing Germany to do so.

The Russo-German pact also made it clear why negotiations between the Soviet Union and the West followed the course they did. They were of value to Russia in securing the best possible terms from Germany, whether from a trade agreement or from a military pact; meanwhile, she was also able to screw up demands on the Western Powers, so that – if the German negotiations should fail – she could conclude an agreement with the Allies whenever she liked, on very favourable conditions. As a sort of bonus, Russia had learnt military secrets from the West and possibly from Germany as well. Germany, in return, received a free hand in the East, and immunity from a serious 'war on two fronts'.

The change of Soviet Commissar for Foreign Affairs in May was perhaps not marked by an immediate shift in foreign policy, although it was certainly a prerequisite for such a shift; Litvinov, as a Jew, must necessarily be removed if Stalin contemplated a *rapprochement* with Hitler. It is possible that Russia did not immediately lose all interest in concluding an agreement with the West, but desired to explore the alternative possiblity – which became increasingly attractive to her as time went on. Soviet diplomats continued to assure Britain and France that there was no change in foreign policy; and they may well have spoken the truth, to the best of their own belief. It is unlikely that Maisky deliberately lied to Halifax on 22 May, when the Ambassador declared that agreement with the West was preferable to isolation, from the Soviet Union's point of view.[32] Provided the Soviet Union was afforded full equality, Maisky explained, 'the Russians would not prove difficult on other matters'.[33] This seemed to carry the ring of sincerity. Perhaps Soviet diplomats had little inkling of what was in Molotov's mind; perhaps Molotov himself doubted whether the Germans would reciprocate his interest in the alternative conversations. Most likely of all, perhaps the important decisions were taken by Stalin alone, and nobody else knew any more than they could reasonably guess.

The story of the negotiations with the Soviet Union was largely misunderstood by many commentators, both contemporaries and subsequent writers. To some extent, this misunderstanding was increased because of the gradual change which Soviet policy was undergoing during the period. In the time of Litvinov, the Western Democracies were more dilatory than Russia. There were reasons for this delay which were a good deal more creditable than those sometimes imputed; but it is easy to sympathise with Opposition critics who did not appreciate the difficulties, or who thought that the urgency of concluding an agreement overrode them. With the coming of Molotov, the blame came to lie much more with the Soviet Union. The Opposition did not easily appreciate this subtle and gradual shift. When delegates from the National Council of Labour met Chamberlain on 28 June, one spokesman declared that 'the Labour movement was much alarmed at the interminable delay in reaching a settlement with the U.S.S.R.'[34] – implying that most of the blame lay with Britain and France. Whether or not there had once been a scintilla of truth in that view, it was certainly not true in June.

Opposition criticism of the Government was largely based on considerations far older than the 1939 negotiations. A very large number of people in Britain – not only Communists, but democratic socialists, Liberals and even some Conservatives – viewed the whole current of Government policy towards the Soviet Union over the previous twenty years with deeply rooted mistrust. Whether these suspicions had ever had much factual basis is outside our present field of study; there can be no doubt that they had lost any validity they ever possessed by 1939. In a perverse way, they may even have contributed to the effect which the pro-Russian critics most dreaded. Long afterwards, Seeds gave the opinion

> that it was the Labour Party in the House of Commons who constantly raised the suspicions of the Russians against Chamberlain . . . Molotov used to show him, when they met, translations of statements by Labour leaders on Chamberlain, and ask, 'How can you expect *me* to believe that that man is sincere?'[35]

People who thought in military rather than political or diplomatic terms often saw matters with a good deal more clarity than politicians. As far back as April, the Chiefs of Staff had discussed the danger of a Russo-German association. On 3 May – a matter of hours before the fall of Litvinov – Leslie Hore-Belisha, Secretary for War, had told his Cabinet colleagues 'that, although the idea might seem fantastic at the moment, the natural orientation suggested an arrangement between Germany and Russia'.[36] Early in June, Sir Nevile Henderson, ambassador to Berlin, reported a conversation with Göring, at which the Nazi Field-Marshal 'somewhat ominously observed that Germany and Russia would not always remain on unfriendly terms'.[37] As the weeks wore on, this point began to be taken more seriously in Government and diplomatic circles. Towards the end of the month, Halifax pointed out to the Foreign Policy Committee that 'if Germany invaded Poland there would be nothing to prevent Germany and Russia coming to some arrangement with the partitioning between them of Poland'.[38] The Foreign Secretary's strongest argument for acceptance – *faute de mieux* – of

Molotov's tripartite treaty proposal was that it would block an agreement between Germany and Russia.

When the British Chiefs of Staff met on 24 August, it was obvious that most of their military assumptions required radical rethinking, and they promptly sought guidance from the Foreign Office. The answer which they received three days later provides a very good indication of many changes which had occurred. The Chiefs of Staff were told that the Soviet Union

> must be transferred from the category of neutrals (pro-ally) to neutrals (pro-enemy). There is even the possibility that Germany and Russia have concluded a secret understanding for the partition of Poland. The defection of Russia has obviously caused the military situation of Poland to deteriorate very seriously and there is now no prospect of a war on two fronts for any length of time.[39]

There was also much cause for concern with two countries which had attracted much British diplomatic attention for several months. Romania, it was felt, would be likely to compound with the enemy. Turkey caused perhaps even greater alarm. Britain and France had been attempting to secure some kind of treaty with Turkey, which could prove very important for the strategic situation in the Mediterranean, and for possible access to the Balkans via the Bosporus. Turkish help could also prove valuable to deter Italy from hostile activity – or to deal with Italy if she did join the enemy. A large British loan had already been arranged as a virtual bribe to the Turks. The Foreign Office view was that 'no sacrifice on our part' would be 'too great to prevent the defection of Turkey . . . we must be prepared to meet Turkish requirements promptly and in full at whatever cost'.

On the other hand, the Russo-German Pact had a very favourable effect on three countries which had hitherto been regarded as likely German allies. Japan was reported to be 'angry and disillusioned at Germany's cynical repudiation of her obligations', and the 'prospects of Japanese neutrality . . . much brighter'. Germany's treatment of Japan would serve as 'an obvious warning to Italy that she can expect no consideration from her ally when German and Italian interests conflict'. This fact, the Foreign Office commentators decided, 'increased the possibility of Italian neutrality in the event of war arising from a German attack on

Poland'. The prospect of Spain remaining neutral was also 'now much greater'.

The one thing which was clear beyond doubt was that the Russo-German Pact had greatly increased the chance of a German attack on Poland, and a general war thereafter. It represented far more than a switch of alliances by Russia – as many countries had switched alliances in the past. Russia fully perceived that the effect of her action would be to encourage Germany to disrupt the peace of Europe. She had deliberately ranged herself on the side of war, no doubt anticipating some sort of benefit for herself. Chamberlain's darkest suspicions had been confirmed to the hilt. At best, Russia had decided to encourage the 'capitalist Powers' to tear one another to pieces, in the hope of gaining from their mutual destruction. At worst, Stalin was now preparing to hunt alongside Hitler.

5 Hopes Forlorn

'I am afraid it is inevitable that the difficulty of three or four Powers reaching clear and definite decisions between one another is greater than reaching decisions in the mind of one dictator.' Viscount Halifax to the 5th Marquess of Salisbury, 25 March 1939 (copy). FO 800/315, fo. 68 seq.

Although the Russo-German Pact came as a complete surprise to the Government – as to the public at large – it had been widely anticipated for months that some kind of major crisis would occur about August or September. It was generally believed that this would concern Danzig and the Corridor; but indications at first were far from certain. In June, some experienced diplomats believed that that particular question was not exceptionally urgent.[1] Evidence gradually began to accumulate which suggested that this particular area would be of central importance when the crisis came. There were charges and counter-charges about ill-treatment of German and Polish minorities; and probably neither set of complaints was wholly without foundation. On 18 August Sir Robert Vansittart, Diplomatic Adviser to the Foreign Secretary and centre of the Foreign Office's Intelligence network, told Halifax that 'it was pretty well decided in Berlin to take action against Poland any day after 25th of this month. The actual dates given were between the 25th and the 28th'.[2]

What particularly worried Halifax at this point were the 'indications that Herr Hitler still believes that we do not mean to fight or that, alternatively, he can crush Poland before we can come in'.[3] The Foreign Secretary rather tentatively suggested a letter from Chamberlain to Hitler as the best way of conveying Britain's intentions. Thus, although the news of the Pact was such a shock, the Prime Minister's next move – which looked to all the world like a reaction to that Pact – had already been planned, though not yet submitted to Cabinet, before the tidings came through. A message

47

was sent to the Führer, telling him in the plainest language that Britain proposed to stand by her pledge to Poland; while indicating rather more delicately that if Germany proceeded thereafter to knock out Poland, Britain would not withdraw from the war.[4]

The message, though well-received in Britain,. was not universally popular in the Dominions. Britain already realised that Eire would probably be neutral if war came. The Australian High Commissioner 'thought the reaffirmation of our position was most dangerous and would only encourage Beck to be intransigent'[5] – a reaction which astonished Chamberlain and 'reduced his confidence' in the Australian representative.[6]

There remained an urgent need to formalise Britain's commitment to Poland. The two countries had agreed months before to replace the unilateral British guarantee with a treaty of mutual defence; but international instruments often take an inordinate time to prepare, and the treaty was not yet signed, although the Poles had been pressing Britain to complete it.[7] On the very day of the Pact, the urgency of the situation was underlined, when the Nazi Gauleiter of Danzig was proclaimed 'Head of State'. Completion of the Anglo-Polish Treaty would remove any possible Polish doubts about British intentions, and serve as further warning to Germany that Britain meant business. A few days later the treaty was signed.

As with the Prime Minister's letter to Hitler, this assertion of intentions met little opposition in public; but that very shrewd and experienced observer, Lord Hankey, noted his private apprehensions. Confessing that he 'shivered' at the news, Hankey added that 'It is quite clear to me that we and the French have no plans which will put sufficient pressure on Germany to relax against Poland'.[8]

Hitler sent a reply to Chamberlain's message, and followed this by a verbal communication to Sir Nevile Henderson on 25 August. There was a good deal about future Anglo-German relations; not much about Poland and Danzig beyond a bleak assertion that 'whatever happened now the fate of Poland would be settled between Germany and Russia'.[9] Neither communication gave any indication as to what redress Hitler sought from the Poles. A somewhat similar communication was sent to the French – this time full of reassurances over Alsace and Lorraine. Perhaps Hitler thought that whatever resolution Britain and France might have formed over Poland could be easily deflected if he persuaded them that he had no objectives contrary to their own vital interests.

On the following day, 26 August, the Ambassador was invited to the Cabinet:

> Asked what was the least which Herr Hitler would accept without going to war, Sir Nevile Henderson said that Herr Hitler would claim that Danzig should be incorporated in East Prussia. He would also wish to include the whole of the Corridor in Germany, but he might, perhaps, be content with extra-territorial roads. At the present time, however, the most pressing question was the minority question; this took precedence over Danzig and the Corridor, the solution of which might perhaps be postponed.[10]

Henderson 'doubted whether there was any agreement to partition Poland'. Next day the Prime Minister indicated in Cabinet that 'he thought that the most the Poles would concede would be Danzig, subject to the retention of special Polish rights and extra-territorial roads for Germany across the Corridor, subject to an international guarantee'.[11] If these two statements were substantially correct, then there was an outside chance of peace – at least for a few months. This argument, however, left aside one feature of the situation. Why should Russia have consented to the Non-Aggression Pact if the upshot would be to make Germany a good deal stronger in the east, while the Soviet Union derived no benefit therefrom? It was surely a fair guess that the Russo-German agreement involved Nazi toleration of some kind of Russian design against Poland.

The immensely confused nature of the situation made the British Government receptive of a new piece of 'unorthodox diplomacy'. Many people in diplomatic circles believed that there were two contending forces in the Nazi Party: the 'radical Nazis', typified by ForeignMinister von Ribbentrop, who aimed at limitless German expansion; and the milder Nazis, typified by Field-Marshal Göring, who were anxious for a permanent understanding with the Western Democracies. That belief gave particular importance to an in-termediary whose existence was revealed to the Cabinet, but whose name was concealed even from them. This story, like so many others, has rather deep roots.

On 31 May, the Crown Prince of Sweden sent a letter in his own hand to Chamberlain, urging the Prime Minister to meet 'a Swedish industrialist whom I know very well personally'.[12] The man was a certain Axel Wenner-Gren, who had lived both in Britain and in Germany, and was a close personal friend of Göring. Contact was made, and in the course of June and July conversations with Göring were reported to Chamberlain; while Wenner-Gren was used to communicate British views to the Field-Marshal. Halifax, and the Government Chief Whip, David Margesson, were kept *au courant* with proceedings.[13]

Another wealthy Swede, named Birger Dahlerus – also an intimate of Göring – now comes into the story. Dahlerus's contacts included Björn Prytz, Swedish Minister in London, who expressed to him the strong view that 'in the event of complications arising between Germany and Poland, Britain and France would not intervene'.[14] At the beginning of July, Dahlerus visited Britain, formed very much the contrary opinion, and communicated this to Göring. 'The Field-Marshal' – so Dahlerus's own account runs – 'expressed his unequivocal wish to arrange a peaceful solution.' Dahlerus then gave his own opinion 'that the only chance of this was for him to have an opportunity of meeting responsible Englishmen who were not in political positions'. When this was put to Wenner-Gren he advised strongly against the idea of a conference involving non-political figures. Göring followed Dahlerus's recommendation, and Wenner-Gren now drops completely from the story.

The conference, which was held in Schleswig-Holstein on 7 August, does not appear to have had much influence on the course of events; but before it could be held, Dahlerus thought it desirable to contact Halifax. The two men first met on 25 July. The Foreign Secretary evinced interest in the conference idea, but insisted that he 'should know nothing of it officially'.[15] Halifax indicated that Britain would do what she could to influence the Poles towards restraint, and hoped that Göring would exercise similar influence on the other side. The following day Halifax reported to Cabinet that 'he had received a message from a neutral who was in touch with Field-Marshal Göring',[16] but did not identify the individual.

On Sunday 27 August, Dahlerus flew into Croydon airport, carrying a message from Göring. Chamberlain met him for the first time, and soon discovered that the Swede had no clear idea of Hitler's demands. Dahlerus conjectured, however, that these would include cession of Danzig and the Corridor, with a few minor concessions in exchange. In that event, Chamberlain told the Cabinet – 'he could see no prospect of a settlement, and that the Poles would fight rather than surrender the Corridor'.[17] While the

Ministers still felt uncertainty about Hitler's aims, Dahlerus remained a valuable intermediary; for he could talk to Göring, and Göring could talk to Hitler. Accordingly, the Cabinet agreed that a somewhat informal message should be drafted for Dahlerus, which he could take to Göring that night; while a more formal reply would be prepared for Sir Nevile Henderson to convey on his own return to Berlin the following day.

On the night of 29/30 August, Dahlerus was again able to see Göring, and then returned to England in time for the conversation to be retailed to the Cabinet at its meeting of 30 August. By then, however, a more authoritative statement had been received from Germany. At 7.15 p.m. on 29 August, Hitler handed to Henderson the German reply, which at last contained a fairly clear indication of the German demands. These included the 'return of Danzig and the Corridor to Germany, the safeguarding of the existence of the German national group in the territories remaining to Poland.'[18] Hitler desired that Polish plenipotentiaries should arrive in Germany in the course of the following day, 30 August. When Henderson suggested that this was in fact an ultimatum, Hitler and von Ribbentrop vigorously denied the allegation: 'it was only intended to stress urgency of the moment when two fully mobilised armies were standing face to face'.[19]

Henderson thereupon communicated the substance of the discussion to the French Ambassador 'and urged him strongly to recommend to French Government that they advise Polish Government to propose immediate visit of M. Beck as constituting sole chance now of preventing war'.[20] Sir Horace Wilson, the Prime Minister's civil service aide, also seemed satisfied with Hitler's reply. He construed the peremptory call for a Polish plenipotentiary as 'acceptance' of the British proposal for direct Polish-German negotiations, and welcomed Hitler's assurance that 'the German Government have never had any intention of touching Poland's vital interests or questioning the existence of an independent Polish state'.[21]

The Prime Minister, however, was a good deal less impressed. He saw 'the demand that the Polish emissary should go to Berlin today' as merely 'part of the old technique' – adding: 'It was essential that we were not going to yield on the point.'[22]

A reply was drafted for Hitler. The Cabinet stiffened the wording a little, and it was duly despatched.[23] Communications were also sent to the Poles, urging them to negotiate directly with Germany.

The Poles confirmed their readiness for a direct exchange of views with Germany, on the basis Britain had proposed.[24] There was some confusion as to who should be the Polish emissary. Lipski, the Polish Ambassador in Berlin, was reluctant, lest he be presented with an ultimatum; Beck also refused to go, 'as he fears being treated like Schuschnigg and Hacha', but was prepared to send someone else.[25]

At 7 p.m. on 31 August, Ribbentrop, 'very ill-tempered', read out the German terms to Henderson. These terms the Dominions Secretary Sir Thomas Inskip described in his diary as

> much more reasonable than I ever thought possible. Danzig abandoned to the Reich, Gdynia to Poland. A plebiscite (on Jan 1st. 1919 franchise). Loser gets a corridor to East Prussia or Gdynia, as the case may be; top of the Corridor to Germany from Marienberg westward; international commission to police Corridor meanwhile.[26]

The terms, however, were apparently designed with world propaganda in mind rather than any intention that they should be accepted; for Ribbentrop refused to give either Henderson or Lipski a document containing them.

In the late morning of Friday 1 September, the British Cabinet met. During the previous twelve hours, many things had happened. Danzig's 'Head of State' had declared the Free City's annexation to the Reich. There was uncertain news about fighting on parts of the Polish frontier, and that Polish towns had been bombed. The Polish Ambassador officially informed the Government that German troops had crossed the frontier, and 'had expressed the opinion that circumstances had arisen which called for the implementation of our guarantee'.[27] Halifax 'had replied that, provided the facts were as stated, he did not suppose that we should differ from the Polish Ambassador's conclusion'. Any remaining doubts about the essentials of the situation were removed during the Cabinet meeting, when Ministers heard of a new announcement by Hitler, indicating that Germany was invading Poland.

Had the moment come for an immediate British ultimatum to Germany? From a military point of view, there was some argument for delay, since civilian evacuation had only just begun; but, as Chatfield observed, this 'was not of determining importance'.[28] Indeed, two of the Chiefs of Staff had indicated to Inskip that they wished the declaration of war to be issued as soon as possible.[29]

Eventually the Cabinet approved a communication to Germany, informing her that unless assurances were given that her aggression had stopped and troops would be promptly withdrawn, the British Government would 'fulfil its obligations' – that is, declare war. This communication had no specific time limit and therefore was not technically an ultimatum. There were two reasons for this omission.

The French Government had indicated to Halifax that they wished to declare war before Britain did – as they did not wish the French people to consider that they had been dragged into war by Britain. The British Cabinet feeling was that the two countries should act simultaneously. There was also a faint hope that a general war might yet be avoided. The Germans contended that their attack had been brought on by a frontier incident – the Poles blowing up a bridge. If this was the cause and not just the occasion of the conflict, was not reconciliation still possible? With these points in mind, the Cabinet decided that the British note should be delivered to Germany at about 5 p.m. When the Prime Minister spoke in the House of Commons, he would be able to indicate that the step had been taken.

The French, however, did not behave like people who were eager to issue their ultimatum with great speed. By the morning of the following day they still showed no signs of desiring to issue any ultimatum at all. Just before noon on Saturday 2 September Halifax telegraphed the British Ambassador Sir Eric Phipps, that 'delays in Paris and attitude of the French Government are causing some misgiving here', and pressed the Ambassador to perform 'anything you can do to infuse courage and determination into M. Bonnet'.[30] At 1.30 p.m., Phipps replied that the French Government agreed that identical notes should be delivered by the respective Ambassadors in Berlin the same afternoon, but

> strongly urge 48 hours from presentation of the note should be the time limit. They say that General Staff would like this in order to enable evacuation of big towns and general mobilisation to take place unhindered.[31]

Bonnet was evidently behaving true to the form which he had shown in the crisis a year earlier.

At 2.30 p.m., just an hour after Phipps's message, a further complication was introduced into the story. Again it becomes necessary to digress and discuss the roots of the matter.

Even before the Non-Aggression Pact, there were signs that all
was not well between Hitler and Mussolini. In the middle of
August, Halifax supplied Chamberlain with current information –
or gossip – at the Foreign Office. The two dictators had recently
met; the story ran that this encounter had been very stormy, and
Count Ciano, the Italian Foreign Minister, had eventually been
'sent to smooth it over'.[32] Italy's manifest desire to keep out of the
impending conflict was strengthened when she heard of the Russo-
German arrangement. Mussolini would count for very little if Hitler
and Stalin proposed to make an alliance. Indeed, one may now
speculate idly whether the sudden switch of German interest from
Italy to Russia was in some way related to the nature of the meeting
with Mussolini. Certainly the Germans were at no pains to allay
Italian susceptibilities. According to one account, the Italian
Ambassador in Berlin 'did not know anything beforehand of the
Russo-German Pact and when he first heard of it did not believe
it'.[33] On the day the Pact was signed, Sir Percy Loraine, British
Ambassador in Rome, was able to telegraph that he was 'now
confident that Italy will not join with Germany if Herr Hitler makes
war'.[34]

In the morning of 31 August, the day before the German attack
on Poland, Ciano telegraphed Halifax 'suggesting that if we could
get the Poles to give up Danzig, Mussolini would use his influence on
Hitler to make him agree to a conference'.[35] The Allies were far
from eager to follow this suggestion, but did not wholly rule it out.
Almost immediately news of the German attack upon Poland came
through, Ciano promised Loraine a public announcement 'to the
effect that Italy will not take any hostile initiative':[36] an undertaking which he speedily fulfilled.

Against all this background we must set the dramatic event which
occurred at 2.30 p.m. on 2 September. Just a quarter of an hour
before the Chancellor of the Exchequer, Sir John Simon, was due to
make an important statement on Government policy in the House
of Commons, Ciano telephoned Halifax 'to say that the Italian
Government had informed the German Government that they still
thought it possible to call a conference with France, Great Britain
and Poland'.[37] Loraine then came to the telephone. That morning,
Ciano explained, the same view had been communicated to
Ribbentrop. He added the opinion that Germany would be
prepared to agree to an immediate armistice, with a conference the
following day. Halifax expressed the personal view 'that the

reaction of H.M. Government would be that the first step must be the withdrawal of German troops from Polish soil'. Ciano implied that Germany would not accept this condition. Halifax promised to speak to Chamberlain immediately on the matter. The Foreign Secretary 'managed to rush over to the House of Commons and stop John Simon making his statement . . . in order to give time to get in touch with the French about the conference proposed and to synchronise with them any action we may decide to take with Germany'.[38]

Halifax soon discovered that Ciano had also been in conversation with Bonnet. The Italian had asked his French counterpart whether Germany could be allowed until midday the following day, Sunday 3 September, to reply to the British and French Notes of the previous evening. The Cabinet record of Halifax's later report indicates that Bonnet had 'reserved his decision';[39] but the Foreign Secretary's private view was the French Foreign Minister 'had committed himself rather further than he was willing to admit to the conference'.[40] A Cabinet was hastily convened, and met at 4.15 the same afternoon.

Halifax gave an emphatic lead on the line he had indicated to Ciano: that there could be no negotiations unless Germany first withdrew her troops from Poland and Danzig. On that matter there was no disagreement in Cabinet. Nor did the French dissent. When Mussolini was told of the Allied attitude, the proposal was dropped. More difficult was the question whether Germany might be allowed until noon the following day to make up her mind. Halifax was disposed to give an affirmative answer, and even to allow until midnight on 3/4 September if necessary. Here, there was a sharp Cabinet revolt. The service Ministers contended, with varying degrees of emphasis, that delay in declaring war would be harmful. Chatfield concurred with them: 'Each day delay meant that the Poles were in a less favourable, and Germany in a more favourable, position.' That was evidently the Polish view as well: the Polish Ambassador, the Cabinet was told, had been instructed by his Government to request immediate fulfilment of British obligations to Poland. The Colonial Secretary Malcolm MacDonald sagely observed that 'the Germans could make up their minds quickly enough on occasions and had been known to ask other people to make up their minds in a very short time'. The Cabinet eventually concurred with those who pressed urgency: as Chamberlain summed up the discussion, 'it was intolerable to allow Germany longer than until midnight 2nd–3rd. September, to make up her mind on these points'. On the other hand, the form of the ultimatum would have to be settled in consultation with France.[41]

The French, however, still proved unwilling to accept the midnight time limit, and the Government statements in the two Houses of Parliament could therefore not give any clear indication on the period of grace which would be allowed to Germany. The House of Lords debate, in the Foreign Secretary's judgement, 'went quite well'.[42] At 8.30 p.m., however, Halifax received a telephone call from Chamberlain

> to ask me to go down to Downing Street at once. The statement had gone very badly, he said, in the House of Commons, people misunderstanding the inability to give a time limit to be the result of half-heartedness and hesitation on our part, with the result that there had been a very unpleasant scene in which much feeling had been shown. I have never heard the Prime Minister so disturbed.

Chamberlain's own later reflections on the incident are also noteworthy. After listing the causes of delay, he observed:

> There was very little of this that we could say in public and meantime the House of Commons was out of hand, torn with suspicions and ready (some of them, including Amery who was the most insulting of all) to believe the Government guilty of any cowardice and treachery. To crown all, a certain number of my colleagues in the Government, who always behave badly when there is any trouble about, took this opportunity to declare that they were being flouted and neglected and tried to get up a sort of meeting.[43]

Inskip's diary records a 'semi-revolt' of Cabinet Ministers 'complaining that the statement was not what we agreed'. He was later able to identify the rebels as Oliver Stanley, Walter Elliot, Leslie Burgin and Ernest Brown (the last two being recorded as 'not so strong'). Chamberlain 'sent for them and they came in looking very sullen'.[44]

The difficulties which Chamberlain had encountered in the House of Commons were counterpoised by troubles he met from the opposite angle at the hands of the French. Their Cabinet had proposed that the two Ambassadors should interview Ribbentrop the following day, 3 September, at noon and tell him that Ciano's armistice proposal could only be accepted if German troops left Polish soil. Unless Ribbentrop agreed to this, the Ambassadors would deliver an ultimatum due to expire at 8 or 9 p.m. the same day. 'The Prime Minister', record the Cabinet Minutes, had told his French counterpart Daladier

> that he could not possibly accept this proposal, since it would be impossible to hold the position in this country, and that it was essential to deliver the ultimatum at an early hour. He suggested delivery of the ultimatum at 8.0 a.m., to expire at 12 noon.[45]

When the French seemed recalcitrant, Halifax told Bonnet that, unless they concurred, Henderson would be instructed to deliver the British ultimatum alone. The French must follow when they thought fit. Bonnet demurred, but had no alternative save to accept the situation.

When the Cabinet met again at 11.30 that night, Chamberlain was obviously still shaken by the evening's experience:

> The Prime Minister said that he recognised the strength of feeling shown in the House of Commons even among those who had been the most loyal supporters of the Government. It was clearly necessary that a fresh effort should be made to correct the position, and he had taken immediate action to this end.[46]

The Cabinet then came to discuss the timing of the ultimatum. They agreed that the space between issue and expiry should be brief, lest Germany launch a surprise attack in the interval. After some dispute about detail, it was eventually agreed that the ultimatum should be delivered at 9 a.m., to expire two hours later. It would then be possible for the Prime Minister to announce both the issue and the result of the ultimatum when the House of Commons met at noon.

Halifax added a tailpiece to the momentuous discussions of 2 September. After the Cabinet meeting, at 1.30 a.m. on 3 September, he returned to the Foreign Office, where he met Hugh Dalton coming out:

> As we passed in the passage, he, still in the House of Commons

atmosphere, said to me, 'Can you give me any hope?', to which I replied, 'If by "hope" you mean hope of being at war, I think I can give you some hope for tomorrow', to which his reply was, 'Thank God!'[47]

What followed thereafter was almost anticlimax. At 9 a.m., the British ultimatum was delivered. It expired two hours later, without a German answer having been received, and Britain was at war. At noon, the French delivered their ultimatum, which expired at 5 p.m., and France was also at war.

6 Adjustment to War

'As someone . . . said lately, "Stalin is now to Hitler what Hitler is to Mussolini".' Neville to Ida Chamberlain, 5 November 1939. NC 18/1/1129

On 23 August, the day on which the Non-Aggression Pact was signed, Chamberlain discussed with Lord Hankey his plans for a broadened Ministry in event of war. The former Cabinet Secretary summarised, for the Prime Minister's benefit, the essential features of Lloyd George's arrangements in the First World War. These turned on a dual system: an 'outer' Cabinet of ordinary dimensions, whose members exercised the usual Departmental duties associated with their offices, plus a special War Cabinet

> showing the following points – small numbers; Ministers without portfolios as far as possible; other Ministers of Cabinet rank to be present when their Departments are affected; Minutes other than those of 'hush' meetings to be circulated to outer as well as inner ring; other arrangements for keeping outer Cabinet fully informed as to war . . .[1]

In a Memorandum compiled shortly afterwards, Hankey added that the collective responsibility of Departmental Ministers for decisions taken by the War Cabinet would remain.[2]

The two men also discussed something of the possible composition of a new War Cabinet. They agreed that Churchill, and the Minister for coordination of Defence, Lord Chatfield, must be members. The question whether to include Lloyd George was more difficult. Hankey felt that he 'had a good mind, but I had heard that he was much aged (he is 76)'. He went on to add, 'I did not trust his loyalty.' Both agreed with the principle that the capacity of men to work together was more important than the exact composition of the War Cabinet. Although the Foreign Secretary had not been a

full member of the earlier War Cabinet, Chamberlain insisted that
Halifax, who 'meant so much to him',[3] must belong. By contrast,
the Prime Minister wished to exclude the current Home Secretary,
Sir Samuel Hoare. In later discussions with men close to Chamberlain, Hankey discovered that Hoare 'had been very difficult lately'.[4]
There was some discussion about a possible representative from the
Dominions, but the two men could not agree on a suitable
nomination. Hankey was asked 'not to commit [himself] to any
definite war appointment', although there was no more positive
intimation at this stage that he might be invited to serve in the War
Cabinet. Perceiving the hint, Hankey noted that if an invitation
were later issued he 'could hardly refuse on patriotic grounds' –
though he disliked accepting responsibility for the consequences of
the Government's Polish policy, of which he had disapproved from
the start.

Little more could be done about Cabinet planning for some time.
When the Cabinet met on 1 September, however, and heard news of
the invasion of Poland, Chamberlain extracted from his colleagues
the undertaking to surrender their seals of office if war came, so that
he could remodel the Government.

Later in the day Churchill was informed of the Prime Minister's
proposals for the War Cabinet. He appears to have made no
difficulties about joining himself, but was somewhat perturbed
about its overall composition. After a night's reflection, he wrote to
the Prime Minister:

> Aren't we a very old team? I make out that the six you mentioned
> to me yesterday aggregate 386 years, or an average of over 64!
> Only one year short of Old Age Pension! If however you added
> Sinclair (49) and Eden (42) the average comes down to $57\frac{1}{2}$.[5]

The correspondence suggests that Chamberlain did not propose to
incorporate any Labour or Liberal members into the War Cabinet.
On the other hand, he certainly wished to have some of them in the
'outer' Cabinet, and the Labour Party at any rate had long
appreciated that some kind of approaches would be made. On 24
August, the matter had been discussed at Labour's Parliamentary
Executive Committee. Hugh Dalton indicated that 'I assume no-
one is committed, or will commit himself to this without authority
from the Party'.[6] Arthur Greenwood, the Acting Leader during
Attlee's illness, reassured him, and Dalton was able to record that

'the meeting was . . . unanimous in my sense'. These views were affirmed at the general meeting of the Parliamentary Labour Party immediately afterwards, and on the following day at a joint meeting of the Executives of the Labour Party, the Parliamentary Labour Party and the TUC, Dalton's comment was, 'My present feeling is that we should decline participation in Government if war came – at least at the beginning.'[7]

On 1 September, Chamberlain made the anticipated offer of a Cabinet post to Greenwood in the event of war. A joint meeting of Labour's National and Parliamentary Executives the following morning declared emphatically that invitations to join the Government should be refused.[8] Churchill correctly foresaw that, without Labour in the Ministry, 'we shall certainly have to face a constant stream of criticism'.[9] Dalton recorded a discussion with R. A. Butler, Under-Secretary of State for Foreign Affairs, which discloses the thinking behind Labour's refusal:

Having regard to our frequently expressed views of the Prime Minister and Simon, we could not enter a Cabinet to which these two were Numbers 1 and 2. Moreover we should require the influence of Sir Horace Wilson [head of the Civil Service] to be eliminated . . . He asked whether we really attached as much importance to Wilson as this. I said, 'Yes certainly, and I have so told one member of the War Cabinet, and one of my colleagues has told another.'[10]

Reactions among the Liberals were essentially similar to those of the Labour Party. On the morning of Saturday 2 September, Chamberlain told Sir Archibald Sinclair of his approach to Greenwood, and the latter's refusal; adding that in event of war he proposed to issue an invitation to Sinclair of a Cabinet post: but one which would be outside the War Cabinet.[11] Sinclair asked whether the offer was being made to him in a personal capacity – in which case his inclination would be to accept – or as Liberal leader. When told that the latter was the case, Sinclair indicated that he must consult his colleagues.

That afternoon, Sinclair discussed the matter with five other prominent Liberals. The Marquess of Crewe confirmed Sinclair's own conjecture that 'all great decisions of policy' would probably be taken by the War Cabinet. The Liberals would thus be implicated in decisions which they had no power to control. For this reason, it was generally felt that Sinclair should refuse – as in fact he did when the offer was made formally on the following day. Viscount Samuel, who had been Sinclair's predecessor, was more doubtful than the others about the wisdom of refusal, and suggested to Sinclair and Lord Crewe that he might offer his own services without engaging the Liberal Party. They felt hesitation but did not emphatically oppose the suggestion. The offer was accordingly made to Chamberlain, but was refused.

Establishment of a War Cabinet involved other problems as well as decisions on its political basis. In the early afternoon of 3 September, Captain Margesson, Chief Government Whip, told his Liberal counterpart Sir Percy Harris that it was proposed to appoint six members: Chamberlain, Halifax, Simon and Chatfield – who would all retain their old portfolios – plus Winston Churchill and Lord Hankey, who would both be without Departmental responsibilities. This corresponds quite closely with the arrangement Chamberlain and Hankey had been discussing some time earlier.

When the list was eventually announced, some hours later, it had grown from six to nine, and Churchill had acquired the Admiralty. Various explanations were offered, which are not mutually exclusive. While matters were still in doubt, Hore-Belisha, Secretary for War, complained to Sinclair about the omission of the service Ministers.[12] One conjecture was that Sir Kingsley Wood, the Air Minister, and a man with more influence than Hore-Belisha, seconded his colleague's complaint and prevailed upon the Prime Minister to include them both. To avoid overloading the War Cabinet by bringing in someone else to represent the Navy, Chamberlain gave Churchill his 1914 portfolio of the Admiralty. Once the number had been brought to eight, it was impossible to exclude the claims of Sir Samuel Hoare, who had served for many years as a senior Minister. Margesson gave another explanation for Churchill receiving the Admiralty: 'the feeling that he would be a very dangerous member of the Cabinet if he was left to roam over the whole field of policy and it would be much safer to give him a job of work to get his teeth into'. The Chief Whip also thought that Hankey had been included 'to keep (Churchill) in order'.[13]

Eden entered the 'outer' Cabinet, at the Dominions Office. Inskip, whom he displaced, took the Woolsack as Viscount Caldecote. This was technically a promotion, but the new Lord Chancellor resented Chamberlain's way of effecting the change –

noting in his diary, 'I shall be glad to be out of his inner circle'.[14] Three members of the old Cabinet – Runciman, Maugham and Burgin – were dropped altogether, and several others changed posts. One of the junior appointments was of some future signifance. Lloyd George's son Gwilym, who sat as a Liberal, became Parliamentary Secretary to the Board of Trade, and was thus the only member of the Opposition Parties to enter the Government. Neither his father nor Sinclair objected.[15]

No less vital to the prosecution of the war than any change in Britain was a change at the French Foreign Office. Sir Alexander Cadogan, writing for the Foreign Office, expressed to the British Ambassador in Paris an exceedingly unfavourable view of Bonnet.[16] 'What we should like, of course, to do,' observed Cadogan, 'is to take discreet measures with the object of getting Bonnet removed from office and ensuring that the Quai d'Orsay is placed in charge of an honest man.' Phipps exerted the influence asked of him, and a week or so later Daladier himself took over the post. This was the second time in less than two years that the British Ambassador played a part in dislodging a French Foreign Minister, and his action was evidently appreciated at Whitehall. Phipps – to his bitter resentment – was in process of being retired; but very soon after Bonnet's displacement he received a request to postpone his retirement – which, in the event, he refused to do.[17]

When Britain declared war on Germany, the Colonial Empire and India automatically entered on her side. Australia, Canada and New Zealand promptly joined of their own volition. In South Africa, Prime Minister Hertzog had wished to keep his country out of the war, but in the last few days of peace there was growing evidence that he would fail: a view sustained by later events. General Smuts carried an amendment in the Union Parliament to the effect that the country should sever relations with Germany. The majority .was greater than anticipated. On 6 September, notification was officially given that South Africa was at war with Germany.[18] Eire, which still ranked as a Dominion, was more reluctant. On 31 August Prime Minister De Valera confirmed to the German Ambassador that his country would be neutral – adding, however, that Eire could not be used 'for propaganda purposes on behalf of Germany or as a base for German action'.[19]

The course of war in Poland was disastrous. On 4 September the Chief of the Imperial General Staff still felt that 'the crushing of

Poland by Germany in a few weeks was most improbable',[20] but a couple of days later was forced to admit that the situation there 'had deteriorated very rapidly'.[21] On the same day the *Corps diplomatique* in Poland was advised to withdraw from Warsaw to Krzemieniec, close to the Russian frontier. By 10 September, Chamberlain was writing privately that 'Poland is being rolled up much faster than our people had anticipated',[22] and a week later that 'Poland is almost finished now'.[23]

On Sunday 17 September, the last chance of prolonged Polish resistance was destroyed by an invasion from Russia. The same day the Polish Government, presumably fearing that the Russians would soon cut off any possible retreat, fled into Romania. The British War Cabinet – who apparently did not all know of the secret protocol to the Anglo-Polish Treaty – heard with evident relief that the United Kingdom was not under an international obligation to declare war on the Soviet Union,[24] and that the French Government took a similar view of its own position. A statement attributed to R. A. Butler, Parliamentary Under-Secretary at the Foreign Office, indicated that the Poles had no desire that Britain should do so.[25]

The Russian invasion of Poland, like most transgressions of international frontiers, received its 'justification' from the aggressor – indeed, various kinds of justification were provided for different ears. Four days before the invasion, *Pravda* – presumably with the intention of preparing domestic opinion in the Soviet Union – published stories of most dubious authenticity concerning alleged peasant revolts in various parts of the *kresy* – Polish Ukraine and Polish White Russia.[26] On the occasion of the invasion itself, the Russians provided a different explanation for British diplomats:

> that there was no proper Government in Poland with whom they could get in touch and that, without abandoning their neutral attitude, they felt compelled to protect the interests of White Russian and Ukrainian minorities in Poland.[27]

When the invasion was more or less complete, Maisky gave another explanation to ex-President Benes of Czechoslovakia. The rapidity of the German advance was thought by the Soviet Government to be a 'threat to their security', and the decision to occupy the *kresy* was taken 'without reference to the German Government'. The

Soviet Government, Maisky assured him, 'proposed to use their influence to secure the establishment in Poland of a new Polish Government protected from German domination'.[28] Whether the Russians were equally keen that it should be protected from their own domination is perhaps another matter.

How far the Poles engaged the Russians was at this stage far from clear to the British Government. A diplomatic report of 18 September reported fighting along the whole length of the Polish-Soviet frontier;[29] but a later account from Maisky claimed that the Russian advance 'had been carried out in a peaceful and orderly manner'.[30] A further diplomatic report suggested that in any event the aftermath was grim:

> Several hundred arrests, already made by OGPU, including bourgeoisie and Trotsky communists (Jews), many of whom have been shot . . . Anti-Semitism . . . directed particularly against Jewish shopkeepers is noticed among the Red Army.[31]

A report as late as 26 September spoke of the Poles still resisting the invasions at three centres, and made special reference to the 'great determination' exhibited by the Jewish population in defence of the capital.[32] Next day, however, Warsaw fell to the Germans, and the last Polish strongholds capitulated not long afterwards.

During the period of Polish resistance, and in the immediate aftermath, various enquiries were held in Britain and France to discover the cause of the unexpectedly rapid collapse. The picture which emerged suggested that the weakness lay not in one place only, but in many. It had long been generally realised that the Polish Army was short of heavy artillery, tanks and aircraft. Count Raczynski, Polish Ambassador in London, gave a graphic account of the effect produced by the German assault: 'Sometimes more than a thousand tanks are advancing together "like an armada", with crushing support from the air . . . "We cannot move one soldier or one cart in daytime without being seen".'[33] In the first few weeks of war, it was widely believed that the Polish air force had been obliterated, much of it on the ground, almost immediately after the German attack. That view was later confuted. The British interpretation suggested that

> The real trouble was that the whole system of communications broke down. Half the Polish Air Force was never in action, and

never got any orders. [Pilots exhibited] great bravery and skill but had to fly about on their own and find their own targets! They never knew where their High Command had got to. Both telephone and wireless communications broke down completely.[34]

This criticism of the High Command – and, indeed, of the whole planning of Polish defence – was reinforced by information from the French Ambassador in Warsaw, Leon Noel. Some of his stories do not seem to be corroborated elsewhere, and must be treated with a measure of doubt; but nevertheless the account which he gave to Daladier, and which soon came into British hands, deserves attention.[35] According to Noel, the Polish army was short not only of heavy and expensive equipment, but also of much simpler items like uniforms, rifles, machine guns and light artillery. Poland had 3 million trained men, with the necessary complement of officers and NCOs; yet 'the number of troops actually employed was probably barely a million'. To a much smaller extent, the many ethnic differences within Poland may have contributed to the speed of the country's collapse. In Lwow, Ukrainians are said to have fired on a Polish artillery regiment. In parts, at least, of the *kresy*, the Poles 'had not called up troops from the minority sections. For example, in one village in Wolhynia, whose population is 3000, only eight had been mobilised'. Yet against all this, there is one matter on which there seems no doubt all; the almost universal heroism of those Polish forces who did see action.

There were many grounds for recrimination about the part played by the Western Allies before and during the Polish *débâcle*. The Poles complained that their urgent requests for substantial loans in the last months of peace had been largely ignored. Nor had plans been prepared for action in the west. Taxed on this subject in the early days of war, Churchill 'replied that if he were not now a member of the War Cabinet he would certainly have much to say on this line, but "I have signed on for this voyage, and I cannot use such arguments now".'[36]

When war came, Churchill certainly pressed for 'every means possible' to relieve pressure on Poland. 'This', he pleaded to the Cabinet on 4 September, 'could be done by operations against the Siegfried Line, which is at present thinly held. The burden of the operations would fall on the French Army and our Air Force.'[37] He went on to urge that the Chiefs of Staff should 'make immediate contact' with the French military leader, General Gamelin, 'to discover the French Army Plan and the best means by which our Air Striking Force could cooperate'.

The visit was made next day, and the two Chiefs of Staff concerned reported back to the War Cabinet. The French had 'no air plan other than limited operations in cooperation with the general plan of the French Army'.[38] Gamelin proposed gradually to move up to the Maginot Line, and thereafter to send out reconnaisances in force to test the strength of the opposing Siegfried Line. 'If, happily, a breakthrough of the Siegfried Line could be achieved, then we should throw everything in to exploit the success, including a strong force of bombers.' Even at this stage, however, Gamelin had 'no illusions as to the chance of Polish resistance being prolonged; this was ruled out'. A week later, an indication of French activity in the west was provided by a report given by Daladier to Chamberlain. German soldiers captured during some minor foray were said not to realise that their country was at war with Britain and France.[39] This is perhaps difficult to believe, but symbolic.

British activity during the invasions of Poland was not much more impressive. The only material dropped from the air was propaganda leaflets, which were solemnly delivered night by night, and formed a topic of recurring discussion in the War Cabinet. In the view of Lord Hankey's son, who was serving with the British Embassy in Poland, 'In Poland everybody thinks it inconceivable that we should not be bombing hell out of the Germans. I don't think anything except retaliation will impress them . . . As for dropping pamphlets, it just makes one's blood boil!'[40] On 13 September, Dalton saw Churchill more or less officially, to complain of the failure to render effective help to the Poles, either directly or indirectly. Why, for example, had air action not been taken against military objectives in West Germany? Churchill replied that a British assault on Germany would be likely to provoke attacks on British aircraft factories, while defensive measures, such as sandbagging, were not complete. 'Further,' he went on,

It is most desirable in order to influence American opinion *que Messieurs les Assassins commencent.* Even if you aim at military objectives, 'there is always a splash' and some women and children are sure to be hit. If we can, let us ensure that the first women and children to be hit are British and not German.

Such were the arguments.

Whether British air raids on Germany would have been valuable or not during the period that Poland was fighting, they could scarcely have proved decisive. The only kind of Allied action which could substantially have prolonged Poland's survival was a major land attack on the Western Front, and the decision on that matter necessarily lay with France.

As Poland's position became increasingly desperate, the en-quiries which the British War Cabinet made of the French became less concerned to produce a particular course of action, and more designed to elicit information, both about France's own intentions, and about what action the French anticipated from Germany. On 15 September, the War Cabinet was told that Gamelin had now decided that the Germans were likely to make some major attack in the West in about a month's time, and 'was anxious to defend himself in the Maginot Line and not to have more troops in front of that line than he could quickly withdraw'.[41] Churchill was profoundly sceptical; he did not believe that the Germans would attempt an offensive so late in the year, and doubted whether the French believed it either: 'If Gamelin does not want to do anything large this autumn, it would be quite natural for him to say that of course the French Army must take into consideration the possibi-lities of a German offensive.'[42] Gamelin's guesses – or reported guesses – of where the German attack would be most likely to fall also vacillated considerably. Two or three weeks later the British Chiefs of Staff were complaining of 'what seemed to be frequent changes in General Gamelin's idea of the German plan'.[43] What-ever Gamelin thought, the French obviously had no intention of making any kind of attack for a very long time. Halifax told the Cabinet of a statement attributed to Gamelin 'to the effect that he would not operate any offensive operations until a third of the forces in France were British'.[44] As current thinking suggested that a full year would elapse before so many as twenty British divisions were ready,[45] this date was for practical purposes the Greek Kalends. If Bonnet's diplomacy could not keep France from declaring war, then Gamelin's strategy would try to ensure that she did as little fighting as possible.

For all the confusion on military matters, there was one question on which British observers were mostly correct in their forecast: that Hitler's first major action after the destruction of Poland would not be a military attack at all, but what was called a 'Peace Offensive'.

'If I were in Hitler's shoes,' wrote Chamberlain on 22 September,

> I think I should let the present menacing lull go on for several
> weeks and then put out a very reasonable offer. It's no use crying
> over spilt milk. You couldn't get Russia out of Poland even if you
> did me. We have no quarrel with you and are quite ready to settle
> down as good Europeans . . .[46]

'Such a specious appeal', added the Prime Minister, 'might be most
difficult to resist though I am certain we ought to reject it.'

The War Cabinet Minutes of 16 October record the 'general
view' of the Ministers that 'public opinion in the country was
practically unanimous in support of the government's war policy'.[47]
The exceedingly poor showing made by those by-election candidates who stood on an anti-war platform suggests that this was
true for the population as a whole; yet nevertheless there existed a
quite substantial number of individuals who had evident reservations on the matter for very disparate reasons, who might
embarrass the Government considerably if a well-angled 'Peace
Offensive' were launched. There were extreme pacifist bodies like
the Peace Pledge Union, which objected on principle to all wars in
any circumstances. From the Government's point of view, such
people were certainly not among the more dangerous critics.
Vansittart was worried about an Anglo-German organisation,
known as The Link, which had existed before the war. Its leaders –
said to include 'Admiral Barry, Carroll, an Australian with a Nazi
wife, and Professor A. P. Lowrie'[48] were scarcely well-known public
figures, and their influence (if any) would turn mainly on the access
which they might have to important people. Those who had been
active in the Fascist movement in Britain were obvious suspects; but
the Home Secretary told his colleagues that 'there was some
indication that Sir Oswald Mosley' [the Fascist leader] was not
likely to take action at present which would expose himself to
prosecution'.[49] In any event, Mosley's strength was extremely local,
and practically confined to certain ethnically mixed working-class
districts in large towns.

More danger lay in the attitude of the Communist Party, even
though it had so long and so passionately preached armed resistance
to Nazi Germany. When Stalin made his peace with Hitler, the
Communists executed a complete *volte face*. Some prominent
members of the Party were not sufficiently athletic to make the

adjustment immediately. On the day war was declared, William
Gallacher, the sole Communist MP, committed himself to the view
that 'the speedy and effective defeat of the Nazi régime' was
desirable 'for a lasting peace for the people of the world'.[50] Harry
Pollitt, the Party Secretary, even wrote a pamphlet advising all
concerned how to win the war. Gradually the message got through
to them that the Party line had changed, and men like Pollitt and
the celebrated J. R. Campbell were driven to make public
recantations of their erstwhile pro-war opinions.[51] Unlike its large
and dangerous French equivalent, the British Communist Party
was a small organisation. There was, however, some anxiety in
Cabinet lest they should launch a 'stop-the-war' campaign, which
could influence the Labour movement. Some attempt was made in
that direction. In December, 'Peace Aims Conferences' were held in
Scottish towns, and attended by vociferous groups of 'Communists,
near Communists and pacifists', who urged 'that we should make
peace with Hitler now, express no condemnation of Russia in
Finland, and cease "collaborating" with Chamberlain'.[52]

Ordinary people who for these various reasons opposed the war
wrote many letters. 'Last week,' wrote Chamberlain on 22 September, '17% of my correspondence was on the theme of "stop the
war".'[53] In three days last week,' he noted a fortnight later, 'I had
2450 letters, and 1860 of them were stop the war in one form or
another.'[54] People who oppose a policy are usually more active than
those who support one, and in that case there appeared to have been
concerted letter-writing campaigns by the PPU and the Bishop of
Chelmsford's 'Peace Council'; yet even when all allowances are
made, the numbers were still formidable.

Some influential people also had reservations about the war. On
12 September Hankey reported news he had had of a meeting
presided over by the Duke of Westminster, which included among
its members the Labour Lord Arnold and the celebrated writer Sir
Philip Gibbs.[55] Most of those present subscribed to a Memorandum
'somewhat pacifist and defeatist in tone'. A further meeting of the
group a fortnight later had somewhat different personnel, including
the Conservative MP Sir Arnold Wilson, and the Buxton brothers,
who had both sat as Liberal MPs before 1914, and as Labour MPs
between the wars.[56]

No less disturbing to those who were prosecuting the war was the
part played by Lloyd George, who had been so full of warnings
about the German menace during the last period of peace. His very

first action after the declaration of war was reassuring. 'The Government', he told the House of Commons on 3 September, 'could not do other than what they have done.' He went on to promise that he would 'back any Government that is in power fighting this struggle'.[57] This statement from an old political and personal enemy drew a letter of appreciation from Chamberlain.[58] On 10 September, however, an article was published under Lloyd George's name in the *Sunday Express*. This showed great contempt for Italy, with especial reference to her part in the First World War. Such an effusion from the man who had then been Prime Minister was highly embarrassing to the current British Government, which was exceedingly anxious to keep Mussolini and Hitler apart, and Halifax raised the matter in War Cabinet next day. Churchill undertook to discuss it with his old friend, but the reply he received was hardly reassuring.[59] Lloyd George's embarrassing communications to the press continued. An article 'reflecting on the Polish Government's conduct of affairs during the German invasion of their country' drew a public *riposte* from Raczynski. Another article was considered sufficiently dangerous to be stopped by the Censorship Department, but was eventually released through Chamberlain's personal intercession.[60] Worse – from the Government's point of view – was to follow; for on 3 October the former Prime Minister made another speech in the House of Commons, profoundly different in tone from that of a month earlier. Anticipating an offer of peace terms from Germany, Lloyd George urged the Government 'that we should not come to too hurried a conclusion'.[61] To many people in Britain, Lloyd George was still 'the man who won the war', and the serious doubts he was beginning to express could well exert a serious demoralising effect. His private opinions in fact ran far beyond his public statements, and in one letter he wrote of 'the utter futility of this ghastly struggle'.[62]

Not only were there influential people who felt doubts about the war, but there were also several quite distinct attempts to engineer peace through diplomatic channels or the like. The Dahlerus saga continued. The ubiquitous Swede maintained contact with British and German officials throughout 1939 and into the beginning of 1940. Various ingenious schemes were communicated for bringing the war to an end, but all foundered on the same rock: the British Government's complete lack of confidence in the proponent's power to establish a regime in Germany which would honour its word.

Another possible intermediary appeared. The German Ambassador at Ankara, von Papen, was thought – perhaps correctly – to be a Conservative of the old school, bitterly hostile to the more brash Nazis typified by Goebbels or Ribbentrop. The Dutch Minister served as a connecting link through whom von Papen's suggestions could reach the British Ambassador to Turkey, and thence the War Cabinet. The suggestions for territorial and economic adjustments in Central and Eastern Europe which came through von Papen were not wildly different from those which came through Dahlerus; but in one feature his suggestions seemed more attractive, for the Ambassador proposed that Hitler should be displaced. Apparently the initial successor would be Göring, while the corpulent Field-Marshal would later make way for a restored monarchy. The matter was earnestly discussed by the War Cabinet;[63] but the Prime Minister – who had known von Papen of old – had no high opinion of him, and in any event it was inordinately difficult to see how the German Ambassador to Turkey could possibly deliver the *desiderata* he was advocating. That stream soon ran into the sands.

For all this flurry of discussion, the Government was perhaps not too disturbed about Dahlerus or von Papen. What was much more worrying was the effect which would be produced when (as everybody assumed would happen) the Nazis launched their 'Peace Offensive' aimed at the British public and at neutral opinion. Should that 'Peace Offensive' be countered, or even perhaps preceded, by a formal statement of Allied 'war aims'?

A meeting of the War Cabinet was held on 26 September – so secret that permanent officials were excluded and no minutes were kept, even for the Confidential Annexes. According to Hankey, the Ministers

virtually came to an unanimous decision that it would be premature to formulate detailed war aims at this stage of the war and that our general line should be based on the following passage of one of the Prime Minister's speeches:–
'Our general purpose . . . is to redeem Europe from the perpetual and recurring fear of German aggression and enable the peoples of Europe to preserve their liberties and their independence.'
That is the test by which any future peace offer must be judged.[64]

The first move in the anticipated German 'Peace Offensive' was made next day. It seemed to carry a new menace as well as the risks of propaganda. Russia and Germany concluded what was called a 'Treaty of Amity'. The two countries agreed on their respective spheres of influence 'following the dissolution of the former Polish State'. The demarcation line ran 150 kilometres east of the 1914 boundary between the Empires. Furthermore; as the War Cabinet was told –

'the Governments of Germany and the U.S.S.R. had agreed to make an effort to bring to an end the present war between Germany and France and Great Britain, and had agreed that, if this failed, they would consult together regarding the necessary measures to be taken'.[65]

What did those cryptic words mean? They seemed to imply at least the possibility that Russia would enter the war on Germany's side.

Hitler's formal proposals were indicated to the Reichstag on 6 October. They followed predictable lines. Poland had been eliminated, and with it Germany's European territorial grievances. There remained the question of the pre-1914 German colonies, and it was necessary to deal with economic questions and the general reduction of armaments. Let some sort of armistice be concluded, followed by a Peace Conference. If, however, these terms were not accepted, then it would be war to the knife.

All this was so familar that the propaganda effect was small. With some relief, Chamberlain wrote, a couple of days later,

Well, the peace offensive has opened and so far we have not suffered damage . . . I have always been more afraid of a peace offer than of an air raid, but I did feel that if Hitler made it himself it would almost certainly be in such a form as to be·plainly unacceptable, and he has justified me.[66]

In the next week or two, signs began to appear of major German concentrations along the Western Front. On 14 October the War Cabinet was told by its military advisers 'that an attack appeared to be imminent. It might even start as early as the following day'.[67] A couple of days later, an attack did come; but it was of limited strength, and its evident objective was no more than the occupation of some strategic ground between the Maginot and Siegfried Lines.

For some time, however, real fears of a major assault in the current autumn persisted. The nature of troop concentrations rather suggested that this was likely to run through the Low Countries, despite their loud protestations of neutrality.

Whether Hitler had planned an immediate assault on Belgium and Holland was a point of speculation; but the reaction of both countries to the real or spurious threat certainly operated in favour of the current aims of German propaganda. On 7 November the King handed Chamberlain the telegram he had just received from Leopold III of the Belgians and Queen Wilhelmina of the Netherlands: a document which made the Prime Minister 'much disgusted for [he] thought it was going to be very embarrassing to us'.[68] The two neutral Heads of State offered their good offices to their counterparts among the belligerents, towards achieving a peace settlement. What prospect they saw for these suggestions is difficult to perceive. Probably the object was rather to deter any immediate invasion of their own countries. Chamberlain saw it that way, and so did Halifax, who wrote privately complaining of the 'smaller states, such as the Scandinavians, Holland, Belgium, the Balkans, who are very frightened and might be expected to go for peace at any price'.[69] This judgement, as the Foreign Secretary went on to add, 'would be difficult to state in any public debate' – yet another example of the way in which people were often unable to put forward their own best case. An appeal from neutrals was superficially more likely to influence British opinion than was a mixture of assurances and threats from Hitler.

The Belgian-Dutch appeal had a limited, but not a negligible, effect. A letter in support was sent to Halifax from Lords Brocket, Harmsworth, Noel-Buxton, Darnley, Arnold and Ponsonby, with an indication that 'we know of many others, including [the Duke of] Buccleuch, who agree entirely with it'.[70] The Prime Minister received a Memorandum supported by twenty Labour MPs, urging the Government 'to offer here and now to enter into conference at any time with enemy, allied and neutral nations who are prepared to cooperate with us in such a conference'.[71] Yet while the appeal influenced some Parliamentarians, it appears to have had very little influence on the public at large. The people had taken a long time to reach the general conclusion that it was necessary to fight Germany; but once that conclusion had been reached it would take a great deal more than two frightened foreign sovereigns and a very mixed group of peers and MPs to shift it.

Yet, in one sense, a strange and temporary peace did arrive in the immediate aftermath of that appeal. The 'well-informed sources' which beset all Governments continued to be active, and stories of an imminent attack on the Low Countries persisted right into the unlikely month of December;[72] but, as autumn moved to winter, that danger receded. In all belligerent countries, warlike activities abated. There were still serious losses at sea; but Britain was still far indeed from facing that threat to supplies which brought her close to defeat in 1917. No major air raids disturbed the opposing nations. By land, the countries of Western Europe settled into that period variously known to contemporaries as the 'Sitzkrieg' or the 'phoney war'.

7 Northern Lights

" . . . another story is told of the Russian–Finnish negotiations. Stalin said to Paasikivi, 'What is the good of your trying to resist us? You have only got a wretched little army of 300,000 men. We should send 3,000,000 soldiers against you." Long silence. "Come on," said Stalin, "What are you thinking about?" "I was thinking of where we could find room to bury 3,000,000 men in Finland.'"*Dalton diary*: story related on 3 November 1939.

The joint announcement which Germany and Russia made on 29 September 1939 was perceived at once by British statesmen to carry a latent threat of war with the Soviet Union. There were various oblique indications which confirmed this danger. On 30 September the British Minister in Bucharest was told 'that a number of Germans here have been told by telephone from Berlin that Russia has definitely undertaken to go to war if peace offers fail'.[1] On 2 October, Sir Robert Vansittart noted that the Russian broadcasts for internal consumption 'are now exceedingly anti-British'.[2] Ten days later, the British Ambassador in Moscow tried to quantify the risk: 'I have not reached the conclusion that Russia is coming into war against us in the immediate future. But I think the chance is perhaps fifty-fifty that she may do so.'[3]

In the period immediately before the war, and during the invasions of Poland, south-eastern Europe had ranked high as an area of Allied concern. A great deal of attention had been devoted during the summer of 1939 to the prospect of securing an alliance with Turkey. The eventual upshot was a mutual assistance pact between Britain, France and Turkey, which was intialled in September but not formally concluded until a month later. This treaty provided for joint action in case of certain kinds of aggression in the Balkan or Mediterranean areas; but it included a proviso that Turkey would not be compelled to got to war with the Soviet Union.

1a. Colonel Beck, Polish Foreign Minister in London, 4 April 1940. (Radio Times Hulton Picture Library)

1b. Conscripts at King's Cross, 1939. (Radio Times Hulton Picture Library)

2a. Molotov (L) and the Führer (R), with interpreter, discussing the Russo-German Non-Aggression Pact, which resulted in complete agreement, August 1939. (Imperial War Museum)

2b. German officers and soldiers in Poland, chatting with the crew of a Russian tank, 29 September 1939. (Radio Times Hulton Picture Library)

3a. Men, horses and carts – German loot secured by the rout of the Polish army around Andrzejewe, October 1939. (Radio Times Hulton Picture Library)

3b. Splitting the spoils. The meeting point of the new boundaries of Germany, Russia and Lithuania is fixed, 1939. (Popperfoto)

4. The War Cabinet, November 1939
Back Row: Sir John Anderson, Lord Hankey (Minister Without Portfolio), Mr Leslie Hore-Belisha (Secretary of State for War), Mr Winston Churchill (First Lord of the Admiralty), Sir Kingsley Wood (Secretary of State for War), Mr Anthony Eden, Sir Edward Bridges (Secretary to the Cabinet).
Seated: Lord Halifax (Foreign Secretary), Sir John Simon (Chancellor of the Exchequer), Mr Neville Chamberlain (Prime Minister), Sir Samuel Hoare (Lord Privy Seal), Lord Chatfield (Minister of Coordination of Defence) (Sir John Anderson and Anthony Eden were not members of the Cabinet, but had access to all meetings.)

5b. Dispirited Russian prisoners about to march off to a Finnish prison camp at the annihilation of the Soviet 44th Division at Suomussalmi, 21 January 1940 (Popperfoto)

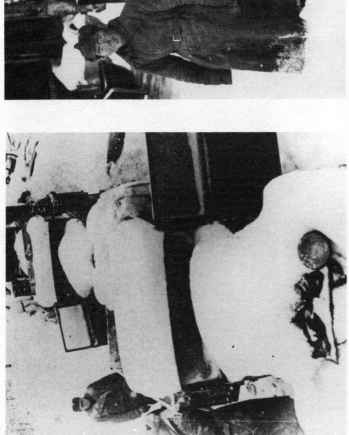

5a. Soviet transport cars captured by Finnish troops (The National Museum of Finland)

6a. Honour among thieves ? (Stalin is said to have asked for German help) cartoon by Partridge, January 1940 (*Punch*)

6b. The Bus – 'Hi ! Driver ! Wake up', cartoon by Illingworth, May 1940 (*Daily Mail*)

7. The Altmark hiding in Josling Fjord, February 1940 (Imperial War Museum)

Clement Atlee (Mansell Collection)   M. Georges Bonnet
(Radio Times Hulton Picture Library)

Edouard Daladier   Hugh Dalton
(Radio Times Hulton Picture Library) (Radio Times Hulton Picture Library)

Maurice Gustav Gamelin   Carl Gustav Emil Mannerheim
(Radio Times Hulton Picture Library)   (National Museum of Finland)

As the Polish war came to an end, Romania seemed a likely danger-spot. In the summer, the Allies had mainly feared an attack by Germany operating through Hungary – with or without support from the Hungarians themselves. The line of demarcation eventually settled between the two aggressors in Poland, however, did not give the German zone a common frontier with Romania; and this fact rather suggested that the danger to Romania was more likely to come from Russia. The practical effect of Russian action might very well be the same as that of German action: the mineral and agricultural resources of the country would be available to Germany. The form of the Allied agreement with Turkey, however, would make it impossible to call on Turkish assistance.

On 27 September – before even the conclusion of the Russo-German agreement on spheres of influence – the British Minister in Bucharest reported a statement from the Romanian Minister for Foreign Affairs that his Government 'would not in any way be surprised to receive an ultimatum from the Soviet Government in the near future. Their intention is to resist'.[4] There was some risk that Britain might be involved in such a war – and that danger was not reduced by an astonishing diplomatic omission. We have already seen that the Anglo-Polish Treaty carried a secret protocol, excluding any British obligation if the attack came from Russia. The guarantee to Romania, also designed as protection against Germany only, made no such qualification, and did not distinguish British obligations in case of German or Russian invasion.[5] Phipps was instructed to discuss matters with the French – but was told that 'in the case of Soviet attack we can give no practical assistance whatever to Romania, particularly if Turkey does not join us'.[6] Substantial differences could be perceived between the Western Allies; for the French were a good deal more willing than the British to become involved in the Balkan area. What finally deflected interest, however, was not so much the realistic appreciation that the Allies could not effectively intervene, but rather a switch of Russian interest from south to north. During the brief period of Polish resistance, a few submarines escaped into the Baltic and – according to some accounts – one was refitted at Tallinn, capital of Estonia. The Estonians strenuously denied the story; but Russia nevertheless developed a keen interest in their country. Late in September, the Estonian Foreign Minister was apparently inveigled to Moscow for 'trade discussions'. He was there confronted by Molotov with the peremptory demand to cede Tallinn. Stalin himself intervened and withdrew that particular demand, but on 28 September Estonia was compelled to sign a pact providing for the cession of bases to Russia. No one doubted that the effect of the arrangement was to take Estonia into the Russian orbit.[7]

Almost immediately came reports of large Soviet troop concentrations opposite the Latvian border; and a week or so later, Latvia was also compelled to sign a Mutual Assistance Pact with the Soviet Union.[8] The British Military Attaché in Moscow learnt that the Russians proposed to station 25,000 troops in each of the two countries.[9] In the first half of October, the 'Balts' – people of German speech and culture who had lived in the area for generations – were given the opportunity to return to the Reich, and advised by their own legation of 'the great danger that lies ahead'.[10] Not long afterwards, the German Foreign Office intimated that the Reich was 'disinterested' in the Baltic and Northern States, 'which are advised to settle their problems with Soviet Russia by themselves'.[11] Clearly the Russo-German agreement of 29 September had delimited 'spheres of influence' not only in Poland, but elsewhere too.

Lithuania was treated in a somewhat different way from Estonia and Latvia. After the seizure of Memel in the spring, the Germans suddenly became solicitous for the Lithuanians, and granted them unexpected port facilities in the town.[12] When war came between Germany and Poland, the Germans urged Lithuania to seize the town of Vilna, which had belonged briefly to Lithuania after the First World War.[13] Lithuania hesitated, and it was Russia who got there first.

Thus far events had suggested that Lithuania was likely to become a German rather than a Russian satellite, and informed opinion in Latvia assumed that this would happen.[14] Matters, however, soon took a new twist. A few days after the Russo-Latvian 'agreement', it was announced that Lithuania had also 'consented' to quarter large numbers of Soviet troops – the figure 20,000 being mentioned. Lithuania would receive in reciprocity – if that is the word – the town Vilna. Rather anomalously, that part of the Vilna region where most Lithuanians lived remained in the Russian hands.[15] There was some doubt whether the Lithuanian Government wanted Vilna at all or merely accepted it for face-saving purposes. A British visitor called Vilna a 'large, poverty-stricken and neglected town'.[16] The population was mixed enough before the war: perhaps 120,000 Poles, 80,000 Jews, 60,000 White Russians and 5000 Lithuanians;[17] it was now swollen by 30,000 or 40,000 refugees – largely, but not exclusively, from the broken Polish army. In spite – or perhaps because – of the *hereditas damnosa* they had received, the Lithuanians were as conscious as the Estonians and Latvians that they had been allocated to the Soviet sphere of influence by terms of the Russo-German agreement; and that the survival of any vestige of national independence would henceforth depend upon Soviet tolerance. That tolerance only continued until June 1940, when all three states were swallowed up by the U.S.S.R.

As soon as Russia was certain that she would receive her requirements in the Baltic region south of the Gulf of Finland, her attention was beamed further north. On 3 October, a Finnish newspaper reported that Russia was 'likely to submit "Baltic" demands on Finland'.[18] Three days later, the Finnish Foreign Minister sent for T. M. Snow, British Minister in Helsinki (Helsingfors), 'and stated that the Russian Government had informed the Finnish Minister in Moscow the evening previously that . . . [it would be] useful to discuss with Finland "certain political questions".'[19] On 9 October, a Finnish delegate left for Moscow, and negotiations began three days later. The Finns, who fully recognised the dangers of the situation, had already commenced evacuation of Helsinki and other large towns. In the next few weeks, Finnish delegates on several occasions paid mysterious visits to Moscow, and returned equally mysteriously to Helsinki.

Meanwhile, there was much speculation in the northern capitals about what was happening; for both the Finns and the Russians were acting in a very secretive manner. Maisky attempted to allay British fears, telling Halifax

that he presumed the principal purpose of the conversations with Finland was to prevent the Gulf of Finland being blocked against Russia . . . He had no reason to believe that his Government would be making requests to Finland that the latter should find it difficult to accept.[20]

As time went on, however, it became increasingly clear that Finland was receiving some kind of Russian 'requests' which she did indeed find 'difficult to accept'.

On 23 September, the War Cabinet obtained snippets of information on the subject of Finland. Halifax had recently talked with the Swedish Minister in London, who

understood that the Finnish Government would be prepared to
surrender to the U.S.S.R. two or three islands in the Gulf of
Finland, and would probably be willing to undertake not to
fortify the Aaland Islands. They would not, however, be
prepared to accept Russian bases on the mainland of Finland, nor
any right of Russian inspection of the Aaland Islands.[21]

The Swedish diplomat considered the situation 'serious', but did not
think that Russia would 'proceed to extremities'.

The second matter brought before the War Cabinet was a
telegram dated 21 October from Snow who 'recommended in effect
that in the event of Soviet aggression against Finland we should
either formally or informally declare a state of belligerence between
U.S.S.R. and ourselves'.[22] Snow 'anticipated that the Government
of the U.S.S.R. might be proposing to establish itself in the north
coast of Norway'. With this document before them, the War
Cabinet decided to ask the Chiefs of Staff for an Appreciation of the
situation 'if we were to declare war on the U.S.S.R. as the result of
Soviet aggression against Finland or any other Scandinavian
countries'.

The reply returned was clear. War with Russia in defence of
Finland would only be prudent if this action 'would bring us
accretions of strength from neutrals'.[23] Otherwise, the conclusion
was adverse: 'Great Britain and France are at present in no position
to undertake additional burdens and . . . we cannot therefore, from
a military point of view, recommend that we should declare war on
Russia.'[24] On 1 November, the War Cabinet endorsed this view.

For a time, the situation in Finland quietened down. A couple of
days later, the War Cabinet learnt that the Finns were prepared to
make certain concessions to Russia, but baulked at the demand to
cede the Karelian Isthmus, where they had strong defensive works –
the 'Mannerheim Line' – and thereafter to demilitarise the new
frontier.[25] This appeared to be the only outstanding difficulty.

A week or so later, the situation suddenly deteriorated. On 13
November, the Finnish delegates returned to Moscow. A day or two
after that, *Pravda* began to complain of an 'anti-Soviet campaign in
Finland', and a Swedish Communist newspaper discovered that
'Finnish workers are incensed at reactionaries' attempts to provoke
war with the U.S.S.R.'[26] On 20 November, Maisky gave a British
Cabinet Minister the comforting assurance that 'Russia had no
intention of presenting ultimatum or using force' against the

Finns;[27] but four days afterwards Seeds reported 'Soviet press
continues publishing daily articles accusing Finnish Government of
concealing determination not to reach agreement with U.S.S.R.
behind pose of readiness to resume negotiations.'[28]

This baleful pattern, adhering so closely to the precedents
established by Nazi Germany, was followed faithfully to the end.
Next came the 'frontier incident'. On 26 November, the Soviet
Government alleged that Finnish soldiers had fired on Russian
territory, killing four Soviet soldiers and wounding others. Molotov
thereupon demanded withdrawal of Finnish troops along the
Karelian Isthmus. Two days later, the Soviet–Finnish Non-
Aggression Pact of 1932 was denounced, on grounds that the
presence of Finnish troops in that area constituted an 'act of
hostility'. On 29 November, Russia broke off diplomatic relations
with Finland. The following morning Finland was invaded, and
Russian aeroplanes bombed Helsinki.

On the next day, 1 December, an announcement was made
which, in its own way, was even more alarming than the Russian
attack. Soviet forces had captured a small town, Terijoki, just inside
the Finnish frontier, and had there set up a 'Finnish Democratic
Republic', under one Otto Kuusinen, a Finnish Communist who
had long lived in the Soviet Union, and who had played a
substantial part in international Communist affairs.[29] The following day, there were further press reports in the Soviet Union, to the
effect that an agreement had been concluded between Kuusinen's
'Government' and Russia. Finland – so Kuusinen undertook –
would cede strategically significant territory to the USSR, and
receive in return a substantial slice of more or less valueless land
further north. This was what the Russians had been trying to cajole
the legitimate Finnish Government to do. The really disturbing
feature of the 'agreement' was that it seemed to imply Russia's
intention not merely to acquire territory and bases at Finland's
expense, but also to displace the Finnish Government by a satellite
regime. As Halifax told the War Cabinet,

It was clear that the Russians were out to Bolshevise the whole of
Finland, and, if they succeeded in the conquest of that country,
he, [the Foreign Secretary] had little doubt that they would
ultimately endeavour to edge round and seize the northern parts
of Norway.[30]

The strategic dangers of a hostile Russia acquiring ice-free ports on the North Atlantic are self-evident; but there were also grave economic dangers which will later call for consideration.

At first, the British Government probably expected the early collapse of Finnish resistance. Arrangements were made to supply Finland with token quantities of war material, but nobody seems to have felt very sanguine that they would be put to much effect. After a fortnight, however, the British Military Attaché at Helsinki decided that 'the Finns were doing very well',[31] but spoke of 'the danger . . . from bolshevisation inside'. It soon became evident, however, that internal collapse would not occur, for social conditions in Finland were not of a kind to breed bolshevism. Just possibly, the Russians themselves had been misled on that score by men like Kuusinen. There were some signs that the puppet 'Government' was not being treated with great seriousness by its Soviet masters. Thus, on 13 December, the Latvian Minister of Foreign Affairs told the British Minister in Riga that his government had not yet been 'invited' to recognise the Kuusinen administration.[32]

World opinion was overwhelmingly sympathetic with the Finns. Democratic Socialists, like the British Labour Party and its French counterpart, were particularly anxious to show that they deplored the Russian aggression. The United States had a strong sentimental regard for the Finns 'because' – as Neville Chamberlian wrote privately – 'they paid off their war debt . . . when everyone else defaulted'.[33] The Russian attack 'aroused widespread indignation' in Italy.[34] Apart from Russia herself and the political movements under her control, there were only two places which did not join in the chorus of condemnation. Germany – in contrast with her Axis partner – took a line which seems strangely inept: 'that the Finns had only themselves to blame if Germany had not helped them . . . since . . . they had evinced no sympathy with the victim of Versailles'.[35] The Chinese Press "received instructions to make no comment on Finnish affairs derogatory to the U.S.S.R.".[36] No doubt the Chinese Government thought Russia might still prove of value in curtailing Japanese ambitions, and feared giving offence. In one respect, the tidal wave of world opinion rose higher than the British Government wished. When the League of Nations met, there was overwhelming pressure to expel the Soviet Union. Halifax advised the British representative, R. A. Butler, to try to prevent the question coming up; but added, 'If you fail I don't think you can help voting for it'.[37] On 14 December, the moribund League performed its last significant act: the expulsion of the Soviet Union.

British concern with the Finnish war had originally been mainly of an altruistic character – although, as we have seen, there were apprehensions on strategic grounds about the situation which would arise if Russia thereafter acquired control of northern Norway. As Finnish resistance continued, however, people began to perceive that it might have considerable bearing on the struggle against Germany, and the 'grand strategy' of the war. If – as appeared likely – Germany and Russia were acting in collusion, there appeared no reason why world antagonism against Russia should not be employed as a weapon to damage Germany. This consideration was particularly important in connection with Norway and Sweden – countries which naturally felt especially strong sympathy with Finland, and were fearful that Russian designs might eventually include them as well. The plan to exploit this situation was largely French in inspiration, but was strenuously argued in the British Cabinet by Churchill.

At Gällivare in the far north of Sweden, and (to a smaller extent) in adjacent parts of Norway, there existed enormous deposits of iron ore. Germany was thought to be receiving about 250,000 tons of ore a month from Sweden, and about 50,000 tons from Norway.[38] Quantities of this ore also passed to Britain; but Britain, unlike Germany, had alternative sources. 'The cutting off of supplies of Swedish ore', declared Churchill to the War Cabinet on 22 December, 'was worth all the rest of the blockade, and provided a great chance of shortening the war, and possibly saving immeasurable bloodshed on the Western Front.'[39] His enthusiasm was infectious. 'Everyone here, and all the colleagues I have seen, are dead set upon the ironfields,' the First Lord wrote to Chamberlain on Christmas Day.[40] At the first Cabinet of the New Year, the Minister for Economic Warfare was invited, and reported the judgement of his Departmental experts that complete blockage of iron exports from Scandinavia would defeat Germany in about a year.[41]

There were two practicable routes by which the ore could reach Germany: eastwards, via the Swedish port of Lulea (and certain smaller ports) at the head of the Gulf of Bothnia, and thence through the Baltic Sea; or westwards via the Norwegian port of Narvik, and thence down the coast of Norway. Narvik was ice-free;

while Lulea was frozen in winter. Just before Christmas, Churchill disclosed a characteristically ingenious plan to the War Cabinet.

Norway and Sweden must be brought into the war on the Allied side. The way to do it was by exploiting their sympathy with Finland. The Allies would encourage the Scandinavians to intervene in the Russo-Finnish War, and would promise their own support against the likely consequences. Germany would quickly perceive this as a threat to herself, and declare war upon them. Churchill seems to have believed that the situation could be utilised without actually involving the Allies in war with Russia. He proposed that the Narvik supplies should immediately be intercepted. Halifax disagreed with this; but the general idea of an approach to the Scandinavians was backed by France, and the Cabinet concurred in that part of the proposal. The Governments of Norway and Sweden should be urged to support Finland; while – as a sort of afterthought – a less formal oral communication should be made to them, indicating Britain's intention to stop the ore shipments.[42]

The first approach to the Scandinavians was rather tentative. On the same day as the Cabinet meeting, Sir Edmund Monson, British Minister in Sweden, saw King Gustav V. Although the monarch began by expressing the encouraging opinion 'that the *great* danger was Bolshevism'[43] he drew very different deductions from those desired of him. Gustav rated Allies and Germans alike for their culpability in conjuring this menace, which would grow so long as the war continued. We may reasonably conjecture that he was particularly frightened that the new Allied policy would link Russian and Germany firmly together in a joint assault upon Sweden. Polish experience did not suggest that the Allies were in any position effectively to resist attack from either, let alone the two combined, and the Scandinavians had not the least intention of gratuitously involving themselves in a similar fate.

The Allies had obviously been duped by their own propaganda. There was a quaint myth prevalent that every democratic neutral state passionately desired an Allied victory, and was only deterred from declaring war on Germany by fear, or by lack of leadership from Britain and France. The attitude of the Low Countries, now reinforced from the Scandinavians, suggests that nothing of the kind was true. They urgently desired reconciliation between the belligerents; and some of them at any rate guessed that the ultimate beneficiary of continued conflict would be Russia.

When the War Cabinet met again on 27 December, it was
evident that there was a great deal of confusion as to just what had
been agreed five days earlier; and in any event preliminary
indications suggested that Scandinavian reactions would be a good
deal less eager than had been naively anticipated. It was no longer a
question of making proposals about the ore traffic to countries
which secretly desired to co-operate with the Allies. The nature of
these proposals and the manner in which they should be issued must
be deferred for later discussion.[44]

In the meantime, much factual evidence was required from
various experts. The Chiefs of Staff reported on the military
question, distinguishing between the 'major project' of stopping all
exports of iron ore to Germany and the 'minor project' of blocking
the Narvik route.[45] The 'major project', they decided, entailed
considerable risks, but these would be worth undertaking if it could
be proved that blockage of ore exports would bring about an early
German collapse – and if, furthermore, the Scandinavians gave
their assent. The 'minor project', taken in isolation, appeared even
more perilous. Germany would probably react by making 'immediate demands' on the Scandinavians. As the Allies could render
no assistance before March, they would be compelled to yield. The
difficulty of operating the 'minor project' without Scandinavian co-
operation was further emphasised when a British ship laden with ore
contrived to pass down the coast without leaving Norwegian
territorial waters; for no doubt the Germans could do the same.[46]

In spite of these apparently compelling arguments against the
'minor project', the War Cabinet on 6 January instructed Halifax to
present a Note to the Norwegian Minister indicating that Britain
proposed to take action in territorial waters to block the traffic. The
excuse for this was that on certain past occasions Germany had
'turned Norwegian waters into a theatre of war and . . . in practice
deprived them of the enjoyment of neutrality'.[47] A copy of the Note
would be given to Sweden.

The response from both Scandinavian countries was a good deal
sharper than the War Cabinet anticipated. The Norwegian
Minister in London was astonished and shocked. Even if the British
allegations of German attacks in territorial waters could be proved,
he denied that they had been sufficiently serious or extensive to
deprive Norwegian waters of their neutral character.[48] At Stockholm, the reaction was positively sulphurous. The Secretary-
General of the Swedish Foreign Office, 'clearly angry', summoned

the British Chargé d'Affaires and invited the unfortunate man to contemplate what might supervene if Britain acted on her Note:

> The consequences of this step would probably be the German occupation of Denmark and possibly the end of the independent existence of all the Scandinavian countries. He then added, 'I should have thought that the British Government had the fate of a sufficient number of smaller states on their conscience as it was.'[49]

Agonised meetings were held to discuss the furious reaction of the Scandinavians. Representatives from the Foreign Office and the Ministry of Economic Warfare were convened to discuss the wisdom of acting in the teeth of such hostility. The conclusion they reached was the action was nevertheless worth taking.[50] A very different response was produced when Anthony Eden sought to discover Dominion reactions. The High Commissioners were all opposed to the action. 'The only practicable method of stopping the iron ore is to get Sweden into the war on our side,'[51] they concluded. A couple of days later two of the Dominion Prime Ministers gave these initial reactions further authority by cabling their formal recommendation that no action should be taken in Norwegian territorial waters without prior Dominion approval.[52] With these weighty observations in mind, the War Cabinet resolved on 12 January to take no immediate action to stop the Narvik traffic; but to give no indication of this decision to the Norwegian and Swedish Governments.[53]

The Chiefs of Staff nevertheless continued to examine the question of possible military action against the orefields in face of Scandinavian opposition. Their conclusion was emphatic. The operation could not be conducted in time to be worth while, and 'as a practical proposition . . . must be ruled out'.[54] Thus everything seemed to point towards the view that the only chance of securing control of the orefields was through somehow winning Scandinavian approval by active participation in the Russo-Finnish war.

The French, whose sense of realism was never their strongest point, continued to press for action against the Narvik traffic;[55] but also began to conceive other plans designed to turn the Russo-Finnish conflict to account in the war against Germany. The Finnish Arctic port of Petsamo had been occupied by Russia at an early stage of the Russo-Finnish War. Its strategic importance was slight, but appeared to possess some prestige value. The original French idea had been to capture it by use of Polish forces who had escaped to the West; for Poland, unlike Britain and France (and, for that matter, Finland) was formally at war with Russia. They soon moved on to the idea that a Petsamo landing would require more forces than the Poles could provide, and would necessitate co-operation between the three Allies. This action, it was argued, would be

> sufficient to make the Germans believe that our objective was to lay hands on the Swedish ore fields. That would compel the Germans to invade southern Sweden in an attempt to frustrate us. The Swedes would then appeal to us for help, and we could at once establish our base at Narvik.[56]

On what grounds involvement of Sweden in the war would authorise occupation of a Norwegian town was apparently not explained. Nor did anyone explain why the Swedes should resist German pressure to the point of war if the Allies seemed to be menacing their most valuable natural asset.

In any event, the British Cabinet was not impressed by the far-fetched Petsamo project. Britain and France were likely thereby to be involved in war with Russia 'without the advantage of securing a valuable prize, such as we should get if we occupied Gällivare'.[57] A better idea than that was necessary if the Allies were to gain the orefields; and minds turned again to the idea of securing active Scandinavian co-operation in the cause of Finland.

The plan which now emerged was to prepare large numbers of regular troops – officially 'volunteers' – for use in Finland. The Spanish Civil War provided abundant precedents for the deployment of such forces in a manner which did not technically constitute an act of war. As Germany and Russia controlled the Baltic between them, the only practicable route into Finland was through a Norwegian port – probably Narvik – and thence across Sweden. Thus the Allies would be in a position both to help Finland and to dominate the Gällivare orefields. This scheme differed from the abortive December project in that the Allies would be initially employing their own forces rather than those of the Scandinavians. The War Cabinet therefore proposed to approach Norway and Sweden with the offer of 'volunteers' for Finland. Meanwhile, they would apprise the Finns that the offer had been made, so that they could exert pressure on the Scandinavians to comply with the suggestion.[58]

When this approach was suggested to the Dominions, they proved far more receptive than they had been of many past British ideas.[59] On 5 February, the Allied strategy in Scandinavia was examined by senior political and military leaders from Britain and France, at the Supreme War Council. Daladier himself did not press the Petsamo project strongly.[60] Chamberlain, reporting to the War Cabinet, acclaimed the meeting as a 'great success', and recorded that 'full agreement with the French had been reached by midday'.[61] Overall responsibility for the Scandinavian expedition should be vested in Britain, and two British divisions currently prepared for despatch to France should be retained in England in preparation for operations in the northern countries. Once Allied military preparations were ready, Finland

> should be advised to make an appeal . . . to the world in general and to the Norwegians and Swedes in particular, to save them from being overrun by Russia. Thereupon the Allies should demand passage through Norway and Sweden for their contingents proceeding to Finland. If these countries should represent that this action on their part would lay them open to attack by Germany the Allies should reassure them that they are prepared immediately to send considerable forces which are ready in every detail to their assistance.

In the event of Norway and Sweden still proving recalcitrant, the Supreme War Council decided that it might be necessary to reconsider the Petsamo proposal.

Soon difficulties appeared. The British Labour Party was alarmed at the information which percolated through to them. On 10 February, Attlee and Greenwood saw Halifax. Two points exercised them: the danger of Britain becoming involved in war with Russia, and the possibility of provoking German reactions damaging to Finland. The Foreign Secretary assured them that there was no intention of Britain declaring war on Russia – while 'the fear of Russia declaring war on us ought not to deter us from any course of action that would certainly seem wise'.[62] On the second count he gave even more emphatic assurances: 'we had this fully in mind and . . . if we were ever in danger of forgetting it the Swedish Government would certainly remind us'. The Labour leaders were perhaps not wholly satisfied; but Halifax does not seem to have feared any serious repercussions from that quarter.

The Scandinavians, however, were no more responsive than they had been to the earlier project. On 12 February the War Cabinet was told that the Chargé d'Affaires in Sweden

> saw no present prospect of Sweden (and still less Norway) permitting an influx of armed forces through Narvik but that the Finnish Minister had been trying to persuade the two Governments to allow several thousand volunteers to filter through by that route in bodies of about 150 at a time.[63]

A few days later even this prospect vanished, when the Swedish Government made a public announcement 'to the effect that they would not in any circumstances permit the passage of foreign troops across Swedish soil to aid Finland'.[64] A closer examination of the military position was no more encouraging. Even if the Scandinavians could be brought to concur, the operation would be far bigger than had been envisaged. It would apparently require four and a half divisions, the bulk of whom would be needed in defence of Southern Sweden. As Oliver Stanley – who had recently become Secretary of State for War – confessed,

> the whole affair was in danger of becoming an unmanageable commitment. If we undertook a new commitment on this scale, we should not be able to send any more troops to France until well on into the summer.[65]

Meanwhile, Finland was becoming more and more hard-pressed. On 15 February, Chamberlain wrote to Daladier, indicating the 'real and imminent possibility of a [Russian] breakthrough unless we can give the Finns at once the help for which they have asked'.[66] The British Cabinet had just agreed to give much more military equipment to the Finns, and Chamberlain pleaded – successfully in the event – for the French to do the same.

The prospect of somehow bringing large numbers of Allied effectives to the aid of the Finns was not abandoned. On 18 February the War Cabinet reaffirmed an earlier decision to send a staff officer to Finland to meet the Commander in Chief, Field-Marshal Mannerheim, and inform him 'that the British and French Governments are preparing a military force which we will be ready to despatch to Finland after the middle of March provided the Norwegian and Swedish Government would allow this force to cross their territory'.[67] The following day the War Cabinet learnt that French troops would be ready to embark on 1 March, and the British a fortnight later.[68]

As there was not the slightest indication that the attitude of the Norwegians and Swedes was relaxing, the likelihood of this plan coming into effect was surely remote. The prospect of saving Finland was poor; the prospect of securing control of Gällivare negligible.

8 From One War to Another

'[Maisky] could assure me that the Soviet would be actuated entirely by its own interests, that we lived in a period of change, that anything might happen, that in the jungle the strangest animals got together if they felt that their joint interests made this advisable.' R. A. Butler note, 31 January 1940, of interview with Soviet Ambassador. FO 371/24843, fos 296–8

On 16 February 1940, there occurred a fortuitous event which may have had profound indirect consequences upon the course of the war, far beyond any which could have been foreseen by those who participated in the incident itself. During the previous year, the German battleship *Graf Spee* had operated in the South Atlantic against British vessels, and captured a large number of seamen, who were later transferred to an auxiliary vessel, the *Altmark*. When the *Altmark* and a British cruiser sighted each other off the coast of Norway, the German vessel took refuge in a fjord. Two Norwegian torpedo-boats were also in the vicinity. A British destroyer, the *Cossack*, was instructed:

Unless Norwegian torpedo-boat undertakes to convey *Altmark* to Bergen with a joint Anglo-Norwegian guard on board and a joint escort, you should board *Altmark*, liberate the prisoners and take possession of the ship pending further instructions.[1]

Contact was made with the Norwegians, who replied that the *Altmark* had been examined at Bergen the previous day, and 'that nothing was known of prisoners'. Eventually the *Cossack* manoeuvered alongside the *Altmark*, and a party boarded her. A *fracas* ensued in which there were several casualties; but between 300 and 400 Allied prisoners were found and released.

The Germans were predictably furious about the incident; but it also presented grounds of complaint and counter-complaint between Britain and Norway. The Norwegians could protest against violation of territorial waters; the British could argue that the Norwegians had not effectively protected those waters against warlike operations by Germany. At best, their search of the *Altmark* had been perfunctory; at worst they had connived at the presence of the prisoners. 'Norwegian territorial waters,' as Churchill told the War Cabinet a day or two later,

> were being used by the Germans to obtain supplies, to forward munitions to Russia, and for the passage of warships. The whole responsibility for stopping this action rested upon a small Power, which had shown itself unable to resist threats.[2]

No doubt the Germans, reasoning from a different angle, also felt that the *Altmark* incident called into question Norway's capacity, or will, to defend her neutrality.

Even before the *Altmark* incident, plans had been drawn up for laying a British minefield in Norwegian territorial waters.[3] The design was to force vessels plying to or from Germany along the Norwegian coast into open waters, where it would be possible for British ships to intercept them. The War Cabinet had not considered – much less approved – these plans, which looked uncommonly like the old 'minor project' in a somewhat less objectionable form. When Churchill raised the suggestion in Cabinet on 18 February, however, the *Altmark* incident was still fresh in everyone's mind, and seemed at least to provide a fair excuse for action in Norwegian waters. The War Cabinet, however, was far from certain about likely world reactions, and decided to defer decision for a few days.

Next day, Churchill returned to the attack. Granted that the Cabinet wished to postpone its decision; yet preparations for laying the minefield would take five days in any event. Would they authorise him to inaugurate those preparations? Halifax declared that he was 'only prepared to agree to the preparations being started if it was fully understood that, in doing so, he was not giving any measure of consent to the proposal'.[4] On these terms the War Cabinet allowed Churchill to proceed.

The French were anxious to go a great deal further. On 27 February, one of their London diplomats presented Halifax with a Memorandum arguing that the Allies should seize the chief ports of Norway, using the *Altmark* incident as their pretext.[5] Whatever the dangers of alienating Norwegian opinion through the minefield project, this French proposal was open to all the objections which had been raised on military and diplomatic grounds a few weeks earlier, and Churchill resisted it as strenuously as anyone else in the War Cabinet.

While these discussions were proceeding, other developments were taking place in the northern countries. The Finnish war began to change its character. Originally, Finland had not wished to appeal to the Allies for full-scale help, for by so doing she would inevitably be drawn into the war against Germany, and it was difficult to see how the Allies could protect her against the likely consequences. The only other source of substantial aid for the Finns seemed to be Sweden, and it became increasingly apparent that the Swedes would not comply. According to the French Government, the reason was not merely fear of Russia: 'the Reich has . . . informed the Swedish Government that it would consider any official aid from Sweden to Finland as a *casus belli*'.[6] The attitude of the Swedes raised the greatest doubts about feasibility of aid from the Allies, even if Finland finally decided to ask for it.[7] Thus it was evident that Finland would be unable to obtain really massive support from anywhere, and would eventually be worn down by sheer attrition.

Not only had Finland good reason for desiring to make terms soon; so also had Russia. No doubt Russia could defeat Finland in the end, and perhaps she was not unwilling to pay the cost in men and materials; but there were other difficulties. If the Allies were drawn into the conflict on Finland's side, this would tie Russia to Germany. The consequences either of defeat at the hands of the Allies, or of victory as Germany's dependent, would be equally disturbing. Russia wanted what she could get without serious fighting; she was in no position to engage in a general war of external conquest.

The Germans in their turn had good reason to encourage Russia to end the Finnish war. They may or may not have feared Allied action in Scandinavia which might block their supplies from Gällivare; they certainly appreciated that the strains of continuing war in Finland would reduce substantially the quantity of goods which Russia could send to Germany.

Meanwhile, as we have seen, the Allies were becoming increasingly interested in extending the war to the other northern countries. The Finns were not without bargaining power in such a situation. They could point out to Russia that if Britain and France were drawn into the war, Russian would be forced into alliance with Germany: the Germans being the dominant partners. Conversely, the Finns could point out to the Allies that the strategic situation which would result if Finland were annihilated would be exceedingly dangerous for them.

While the Finns had good reason not to apply formally for Allied aid, they could certainly indicate their requirements from the Allies. At the beginning of March, Halifax was told that they needed 100 bombers immediately, and 50,000 troops by the end of the month.[8] Of the two kinds of help, war material was more important than men. Great numbers of Russian troops were concentrated in the Karelian Isthmus and presented an easy target. Aeroplanes could be supplied to Finland even though the Scandinavians remained recalcitrant; men could not. Receipt of war material alone would not involve Finland in war with Germany: indeed, the Germans would probably be glad to see it employed against Russians instead of themselves.

The French were noticeably more eager than the British for intervention in Scandinavia. Britain, not France, would bear the brunt of the campaign, and might draw off the heat of Germany's attack from the French. There were also more personal reasons. Cambon explained to Chamberlain on 1 March that 'M. Daladier felt that he could not maintain his position if effective steps were not taken to help Finland'.[9] Later the same day, further news arrived which cast little credit on the French Premier. When the Finns indicated their requirements of men and munitions in order to keep fighting, Daladier told the Finnish Minister 'that the French Government were prepared to accede to the Finnish request on all points'[10] – with the clear implication that any failure to satisfy these requirements was the fault of Britain. Minutes of the War Cabinet do not usually reveal much passion, but on this score they did:

> It was generally agreed that this was a most disquieting message, and that the French action was a bad example of lack of cooperation. The French were apparently prepared to bluff, knowing that they could throw on us the whole blame for the failure to redeem their promises, as we had undertaken the direction of the expedition.[11]

Meanwhile, another approach was devised, to try to overcome difficulties from the Scandinavians. A new British *démarche* was made, telling the Governments of Norway and Sweden that at a later date passage would be requested. The British plan was to continue discussions 'until the moment would arrive when we could say to them abruptly that our troops were ready, and we intended to come through'.[12] Lord Chatfield later proposed a slight modification of this proposal: that 'test' forces should be sent to Norway, 'and, if they were successful in getting ashore, the remainder of the expedition could follow after them'.[13] It was fairly certain, however, that an opposed landing was out of the question. Even if the Allies were successful in seizing Narvik, further progress towards Gällivare and Finland could be blocked by the simple expedient of cutting off electric current from the railways.

As early as 6 March, Chamberlain thought 'that we should probably not receive from the Finnish Government the appeal we had been waiting for';[14] but discussion continued in Cabinet as to what help could be rendered if the appeal were made. The demand for 100 bombers was considered excessive. Half of that number might perhaps be provided – although the Chief of Air Staff 'could not see any military, as opposed to psychological, justification for the despatch of additional bombers to Finland'.[15] He told the Cabinet that if 50 bombers were sent, it was unlikely that more than 10 would ever return. Winston Churchill and Air Minister Sir Kingsley Wood went further: they 'deprecated sending further aircraft to Finland, since we should thereby weaken ourselves against Germany'.[16]

The diplomatic fencing and Cabinet arguments continued. Field-Marshal Mannerheim, the Cabinet was told on 7 March, 'felt that he had already made his appeal, though it was for bombers that he had asked as being his most urgent need'.[17] This, of course, was exactly what the British Government did not want to hear. A demand for bombers would provide no pretext for Britain and France to coerce the Scandinavians to allow troops to land within striking distance of Gällivare. Halifax, however, was reconciled to the inevitable: 'the right course was, therefore, to send bombers immediately and waste no more time haggling with Sweden'.[18] At last authority was given 'for the despatch of up to fifty bomber aircraft to Finland subject to further consultation'. Meanwhile the Finns would be asked 'for a definite answer within a specified period as to whether [they] intended to issue an appeal for Allied land forces'.[19]

The belated British decision perhaps gave Mannerheim an

important lever in peace discussions, which now began in earnest. The French were appalled. Daladier sent a message to the Finnish Government, urging them 'very strongly not to conclude a shameful peace'[20] – words which must have sounded ironic four months later. The French Prime Minister's message evinced that strange propensity to ignore military realities which had characterised much that he had said about Czechoslovakia in the previous year. As Halifax told the Cabinet, Daladier 'referred to the unlimited support which France and Great Britain were preparing to send to Finland if the Finns appealed for it without, however, making any reference to the difficulties of despatching such a force through Norway and Sweden.[21]

Thus by the end of the first week in March the Finns, the Russians, the Swedes and the Germans all desired a speedy termination of the northern conflict, though for very disparate reasons, and even the British were reconciled to the idea, for they perceived that it was impossible to render adequate help. Only the French were – in the words of the War Cabinet minutes – 'desperately frightened that the Finns would make peace'.[22] For Finland, the situation was desperate in a different sense; as the Minister for Foreign Affairs told Allied representatives 'in two weeks the Russians would have entered the capital; [Finland] could not possibly have held out for the four or five weeks before the Allied help arrived' – even if somehow Norway and Sweden were prevailed upon to allow the troops to pass.[23]

On 13 March, a treaty was concluded. Finland ceded substantial slices of territory, including the town and bay of Viborg (Vipuri), and the whole Karelian Isthmus. Although 'the fear of the resurrection of Kuusinen haunted them throughout the negotiations'[24] the Finns contrived to maintain national independence; there were 'no political conditions apparently and no question of disbanding the Finnish army'.[25] As for the people of the country, the British Minister in Helsinki 'formed impression that Finns are undefeated in spirit and regard peace as an armed truce and will seize first favourable opportunity to regain lost territory'.[26] This spirit would doubtless have been applauded by the overwhelming majority of Britons at the time. Who in the world would have believed that when – less than two years later – the Finns perceived and took such an opportunity, the responses of the British Government would be to declare war, not on Russia but on Finland?

With almost indecent haste, the British Cabinet resolved to stop any further despatch of war materials to Finland, and to unload material which was waiting at Leith docks. They also decided to take 'all possible measures . . . to secure the return of as large a part as possible of the war material which . . . had left the country'.[27] When Halifax and Chatfield saw the Finnish Minister in London the same evening, however, the latter's reaction was

> both immediate and unexpected. He . . . urged that the present peace was nothing but an armed truce, and that to take away the equipment would be a terrible blow to Finland, which might at any time have to resume its struggle with the U.S.S.R.[28]

This view was confirmed not only from Finland itself, but also from Sweden.[29] Bearing this point in mind, the War Cabinet relented to the extent that they would not interfere with goods in transit to Finland, though they proposed later to request return of certain vital war material. The French took a similar attitude.[30] Within a few days, any prospect of early renewal of the Russo-Finnish war receded from serious contemplation; but there was no attempt to alter the substantive decision taken by Britain and France.

Allied interest in activity in Scandinavia did not cease when the justification provided by the Russo-Finnish war was removed. At the first meeting of the War Cabinet after conclusion of peace, Winston Churchill stated the position with engaging frankness:

> Our real objective was, of course, to secure possession of the Gällivare orefields . . . Up till now we had had assistance to Finland as 'cover' for such a move on our part, but we had now lost this justification for intervention in Scandinavia.[31]

Churchill was by no means disposed to abandon an attractive military project for such reasons, and a more tenuous excuse must be manufactured:

> The only chance seemed to be to take the line that our national interests were directly threatened by the possibility of Russia making her way through Scandinavia to the Atlantic. A decision to seize Narvik by force was a very unpleasant one to take but it had to be balanced against the much worse prospect of very costly fighting on the Western Front later on.[32]

Chamberlain objected to the proposed Narvik expedition, though hardly on moral grounds:

> The despatch of an expedition to Narvik would serve no useful purpose. The Swedes would certainly have no hesitation in opposing us and sabotaging their railways if we tried to force our way in, now that the justification of assisting Finland no longer remained.[33]

Halifax seconded the objection: 'The only effect . . . would be to drive the Norwegians and Swedes into the arms of the Germans'. This view prevailed. The War Cabinet decided that the force prepared for the Scandinavian expedition should be disbanded as soon as it became clear that peace would be concluded between Russia and Finland.

The French, however, took a very different view. On the following day, Corbin, the French Ambassador, explained that he had been instructed by his Government 'to suggest that consideration should once again be given to the proposal for the Allied control of Scandinavian territorial waters and if necessary the occupation of certain Norwegian ports'.[34] This rather halted Halifax in his tracks; but after a few days' consideration he decided that 'the French arguments for carrying out this project at the present juncture were not convincing'[35] – a view which was generally endorsed by his colleagues.

Another matter with even wider implications came under discussion between the Allies. During the Russo-Finnish War, as we have seen, there had been discussions between the Allies about the possibility of war against Russia – not primarily to secure any benefit at the expense of the Soviet Union, but as a necessary incidental to the war against Germany. A few days before the end of the Finnish war, the British Chiefs of Staff were quite emphatic on the subject:

> The risk of initiating war with Russia would be acceptable only if it led to a result which might cause the early defeat of Germany . . . As a result of our present examination we consider that there is no action which we could take against Russia which would bring about the early defeat of Germany.[36]

Again, the French took a very different view. In the opinion of

Alexis Léger, Civil Service head of the French Foreign Office, 'Russia . . . would not stop at the conquest of Finland. She would go on to swallow up a large part both of Sweden and Norway.'[37]

Just as the French were disposed to believe that Russia contemplated further aggression against others, so also did they consider that Soviet economic assistance to Germany provided justification for military action against the Soviet Union. A substantial body of French opinion came to advocate an attack on Baku, in the Caucasus, from which Germany was alleged to receive much of her oil. This view received some support in Britain from Lord Chatfield,[38] but Halifax was extremely sceptical of the whole idea.[39] There is little doubt that it would have disappeared into limbo very quickly but for the great interest which the French lavished upon it. What was particularly embarrassing here was that the most prominent supporter of the policy was Paul Reynaud, who also stood out as the most conspicuous French advocate of an active policy towards Germany.

If British opinion was sceptical about the far-fetched schemes for action in Scandinavia and Baku, there was no disagreement between the Allied Governments on the need to regain military initiative. The line of action which appealed to the War Cabinet was what became known as 'Royal Marine Operation'. This was a plan to introduce large numbers of floating mines into German reaches of the Rhine, and perhaps later into other rivers too; an operation which could be conducted by various means, such as sending the mines down French tributaries, or depositing them from aircraft. Adequate warning could be given to neutral shipping on the Rhine before the mines appeared; while devices would be inserted to render them innocuous by the time they floated downstream through the Netherlands.[40]

While discussions were at this uncertain stage, a new complication was introduced into the story. On 20 March, Daladier's Government in France fell. Halifax was convinced that this was 'entirely due to public feeling regarding Finland'.[41] 'It was quite clear', observed the Foreign Secretary, 'that the criticism of the Government was not based on any desire for peace, but on a desire for a more energetic prosecution of the war.'[42] Paul Reynaud, who headed the new administration, felt bound to incorporate his predecessor in the Cabinet: a decision which both he and the British would shortly have cause to regret. Daladier was resentful at his displacement, and sought to turn the tables at the earliest opportunity; while the British Government was prepared to make considerable concessions on matters of military and diplomatic judgement in order to retain in office an administration committed to vigorous conduct of the war.

Britain accordingly proposed a compromise between her own views and those of France in a rather lengthy *aide-mémoire*, which was communicated to Corbin on 27 March.[43] A Note should be delivered to the Scandinavians declaring in peremptory terms the Allied intention to defend and advance their 'vital interests' in the area. The form – and the consequences – of this communication will need to be considered later. The Note was conceived as a prelude to minelaying in Norwegian waters; but no action against the Scandinavian mainland was contemplated.

The Supreme War Council held the following day fulfilled the most sanguine British expectations. The French, who

had misinterpreted our Paper as a manoeuvre to shelve action in Scandinavia . . . had been agreeably surprised that we were prepared to take action at an early date. Possibly on this account the French had been much more accommodating than we had anticipated in regard to the Royal Marine Operation.[44]

A plan of action was provisionally agreed, which would begin with delivery of the Notes three days later, and would be followed up by inauguration of the Royal Marine Operation on 4 April, and minelaying in Norwegian waters the next day.[45] The Baku project, the Supreme War Council agreed, should be remitted to the military experts for study. Perhaps the British Government was not sorry a day or two later when the New Zealand Cabinet declared itself 'much perturbed'[46] at this astonishing scheme.

Soon trouble arose. On 31 March, the French War Committee 'failed to endorse the resolution of the Supreme War Council on the subject of the Royal Marine Operation'.[47] Corbin, in a 'gloomy and apologetic mood', explained that 'the objection had come from M. Daladier on the grounds that the Germans might take reprisals against French munition and aircraft factories'. Chamberlain's first reaction was to retort 'No mines – no Narvik'.[48] He took urgent counsel with Halifax and Churchill, who concurred that the whole plan of operations agreed at the Supreme War Council must now be suspended. A response was duly prepared for the French. Yet another difficulty was now introduced; for the story of decisions at the Supreme War Council was promptly leaked to the French Press: a very common hazard in those days for all diplomatic activity involving France. In the view of the British Ambassador to Paris, 'the leakage . . . was due either to M. Daladier or to a member of his entourage'.[49]

Every effort was bent to influence Daladier. Chamberlain went so far as to draft a personal letter. When permission was sought from Reynaud to deliver that letter, however, it was politely but firmly refused 'on the ground that it would make things even more difficult for him with M. Daladier'.[50] This reaction surprised the British Ambassador; but he was able to report an alternative suggestion from Reynaud 'to the effect that the First Lord of the Admiralty . . . might pay a visit to Paris and, after seeing M. Reynaud, might call on M. Daladier and do his best to bring the latter round'.[51] The Ambassador, however, had 'not much hope that even this would be successful'. Eventually Churchill was despatched to Paris to do his best with the two Frenchmen.

Meanwhile, the situation began to acquire considerable urgency: as Oliver Stanley told the War Cabinet, 'in view of the meeting of the French Senate on Tuesday 9 April it was essential that action should be taken before that date, since otherwise the French Government would fall'.[52]

During the War Cabinet meeting of 5 April, Halifax was called to the telephone to receive a message from Churchill, speaking from Paris. He had failed to shift Daladier on the Royal Marine Operation question. The First Lord later set his own reactions down in writing, in a note for the Prime Minister. The French were 'serious in their alarms about their aviation; and it would be unwise to press them against their judgement'.[53]

Thus were the British Ministers brought to an agonising decision. Should they accept the rebuff, and go ahead with the agreed plan for Scandinavia? The Baltic ice would thaw in a few weeks, and the ore would then be exported from Lulea; so the original object of laying the minefield had been largely frustrated in any event. The draft Notes to Norway and Sweden had been designed with a view to influencing the French over the Royal Marine Operation, rather than with any idea that the action contemplated would have any great effect on the ore shipments; while the diplomatic and military arguments against the move envisaged were formidable.

The argument which outweighed all the others concerned the

political situation in France. 'It was essential', argued Lord Halifax to his Cabinet colleagues,

> to secure cooperation between M. Reynaud and Daladier, for if M. Reynaud fell and was replaced by M. Daladier, it was inevitable that a period of internal difficulty would follow in France. The bad effects which would follow a disturbance in the French political field, coupled with the general psychological position, constituted perhaps the most weighty factors in a very difficult situation.[54]

The War Cabinet accepted this analysis.

Having capitulated to the exigencies of French domestic politics, Britain now found herself in the exceedingly uncomfortable position of presenting Notes to Norway and Sweden. Documents substantially the same as those drawn up before the Supreme War Council meeting were now delivered by Halifax to the Norwegian and Swedish Ministers in London, and by the British Ministers in Oslo and Stockholm to the Scandinavian Foreign Ministers.

The Notes were, to say the least, extraordinary compositions. If they had been designed with the deliberate object of infuriating the Scandinavians, they could scarcely have been phrased more brutally. They began by reciting that the Allies could not acquiesce in any further attack by Germany or Russia upon Finland; that if Norway or Sweden blocked Allied aid to Finland this 'would be considered . . . as endangering their vital interests'.[55] Any 'exclusive political agreement' which the Scandinavians might enter with Germany would be considered 'an unfriendly act'; any Scandinavian alliance providing for acceptance of aid from Germany 'would be considered . . . to be directed against ourselves'. 'Any attempt by the Soviet Union to obtain from Norway a footing on the Atlantic seaboard' would be contrary to the 'vital interests' of the Allies. If the Scandinavians curtailed commercial and shipping facilities to the Allies, 'appropriate measures' would be taken. Finally, and very cryptically, the Allies reserved

> the right to take such measures as they may think necessary to hinder or prevent Germany from obtaining in those countries facilities which, for the purpose of the war, would be to her advantage or to the disadvantage of the Allies'.[56]

Thus, when the horse had escaped, was the stable door banged in the noisiest and most offensive manner imaginable.

The Scandinavian reactions were immediate. The Norwegian Minister in London 'had appeared to be much upset at the terms of the Note. His comment had been that he feared our policy would drag his country into the war'.[57] The Swedish Foreign Minister's first remark was, 'This brings our countries very close to war.' The Norwegian Foreign Minister 'was clearly very hurt' and declared the wording to be 'disdainful . . . the language of a sovereign to a vassal'.[58] The British Minister in Stockholm wrote with gentle litotes to Cadogan, 'I hope that I may be forgiven for saying that the wording of our Note might have been happier.'[59] The transmitters of the various Notes did their best, and with some effect, to allay the worst effects of these missives; but one remains astonished at their gratuitously offensive tone. The Scandinavians could surely be excused for reading them to imply that the Allies proposed an early invasion of their countries in order to secure the orefields.

At 4.30 a.m. on Monday 8 April, Britain began to lay mines in Norwegian territorial waters. Norway vigorously protested; but far more spectacular events next day thrust that protest, and the action which had occasioned it, into limbo.

9 Things Fall Apart . . .

'Il faut voir grande ou renoncer à faire la guerre. Il faut agir vite ou perdre la guerre.' Paul Reynaud to Neville Chamberlain, 26 April 1940 (copy). PREM 1/419

On 3 April 1940, the day before those astonishing messages to Norway and Sweden, several important Government changes were announced. Lord Chatfield was dropped from the War Cabinet, and Sir Samuel Hoare exchanged places with Sir Kingsley Wood – the former thus becoming Secretary for Air and the latter moving to the more or less non-Departmental post of Lord Privy Seal. A newcomer, Lord Woolton, became Minister of Food: an office which he would occupy with much popularity for a long time. The most important innovation was the appointment of Winston Churchill to chairmanship of a body sometimes called the Military Co-ordination Committee but (to the confusion of the historian) occasionally designated War Co-ordination Committee, or even by other titles. The Prime Minister was very pleased:

> The changes I have made are the final results of long cogitation and frequent consultation with others. I am satisfied that they are all likely to be improvements and moreover have succeeded in carrying them through without a cross word from any of those concerned.[1]

Churchill, who retained his old portfolio of the Admiralty, was said to be 'in the seventh heaven'. Commentators were uncertain of the scope given to him by the new appointment. Some wrongly thought that he was *de facto* Minister of Defence, with power to override the service Departments. Nevertheless, he was generally treated as the individual carrying most personal authority in all matters concerning Britain's conduct of the war.

Almost immediately, the new Chairman of the Military Co-ordination Committee found himself in charge of matters far more complex than the Norwegian minelaying. There had been ample warning that Germany would follow that minelaying by military action in Scandinavia. Reports of German concentrations were received from 26 March onwards, and in increasing numbers.

Just after midnight on 5/6April, the British Minister in Copenhagen telegraphed the substance of American reports 'that last night Herr Hitler gave orders to send one division in ten ships moving unostentatiously at night to land at Narvik April 8th. occupying Jutland same day but leaving Sweden'.[2] Diplomatic papers are stuffed with so many warnings that it would be excessively imprudent, and perhaps impossible, to act on all of them; but this information was taken very seriously, and on 7 April the report of an impending German invasion of Scandinavia was communicated to the Home Fleet.[3]

The minelaying, as we have seen, began in the early morning of 8 April. About twenty-four hours later, the German invasion of Scandinavia commenced. In Reynaud's view, not only were troops collected, but ships actually set sail, before the minelaying took place.[4] The whole of Denmark – not merely Jutland – was occupied without resistance in a few hours; and in the course of the first day the principal Norwegian ports were also seized. A puppet Government was set up in Oslo under the Norwegian Nazi, Quisling, whose name added an odious word to the English language. King Haakon refused demands to place his country under German military occupation, and to install Quisling's administration as the lawful Government of the country. There was, however, considerable initial doubt about the likely duration of Norwegian resistance. On 10 April, Chamberlain warned his Cabinet colleagues that the 'prospect had to be faced that the Norwegian Government might capitulate to Germany at any moment'.[5] There was no question from the start of the Norwegians providing much resistance on their own account. A paper submitted to the War Cabinet a few days before the invasion[6] recorded that 'In peace the Norwegian army only exists for 34 days in the year. . . . For the remainder . . . the army is reduced to a small permanent cadre of some 2,000 men . . . The present strength (March 1940) . . . is believed to be about 20,000 of whom half are in the north.' Whatever the Norwegian Government or army might do, however, the Allied Governments were determined to fight the Germans in Norway.

On the day of the German invasion, the Supreme War Council met. Practically the only certain information was that the Germans had occupied various southern ports. Reynaud 'had emphasised the vital importance of securing Narvik'.[7] It was still not known, however

> whether or not Narvik was occupied by the Germans and it had been decided that while all preparations should be made for operations against Norwegian ports the objectives against which they should be employed should be decided when the situation was clearer.[8]

The French – so the Prime Minister reported – 'had assured us that their contingent was ready and willing to participate in an expedition.'[9]

First attention was therefore directed at Narvik, although it became clear almost immediately after the Council meeting that the Germans had in fact occupied the town. It appeared that the invaders would have difficulty in reinforcing their troops, since Narvik's only good land communications were with Sweden. On 11 April, the War Cabinet was informed that the advance party of a British expedition had already sailed for Narstad, a small Norwegian naval base about fifteen miles to the north; and they would shortly be followed by a larger contingent which would presumably attempt to seize Narvik.[10] This news, however, proved premature. Even more erroneous were the sensational tidings reported in the press the following day that Britain had recaptured Bergen and Trondhjem.

As the situation gradually clarified, it became apparent that the Germans were by no means in complete control of Norway; there were important places in various parts of the country which were still in Norwegian hands. Of those places which Germany had captured, the Scandinavians were particularly anxious to regain Trondhjem. The Swedes urged the 'vital importance' of the town.[11] A 'special message' was sent to Churchill through the British Legation at Stockholm: 'Most important that Trondhjem be recaptured forthwith or both Norway and Sweden will completely lose faith in us.'[12] Writing a few weeks later, Chamberlain was even more blunt about the situation. The Norwegians had given Britain to understand that unless the attempt were made to recapture Trondhjem 'they would make terms and that would put both countries into German hands at once'.[13] The French War Committee, which had spoken so strongly and so recently for Narvik, also decided that Trondhjem was 'now the vital point'.[14]

The Allies struck at both targets. Churchill told the Cabinet on 14 April of current plans. 'Operation Rupert' would aim principally at Narvik, 'Operation Maurice' at Trondhjem. In both cases there was much initial doubt about the strength of German defences, and at first it appeared possible that landings might be made in the towns themselves. It was later decided that the Trondhjem attack should involve two landings – one at Namsos, about eighty miles to the north, and the other at a similar distance to the south. Another landing should be made at some distance from Narvik. The first landings at Namsos and Narvik would be made later that day by British troops alone; the landing to the south of Trondhjem was eventually made at Aandalsnes a few days later, with French troops also participating.

The three landings were successful. On 19 April the War Cabinet was told that 'approximately 8,000 men had now been put ashore without any casualties'.[15] As the scheme developed, it was proposed eventually to land 50,000–60,000 men in Scandinavia, half of whom would be French.[16]

It soon became clear, however, that German forces in Norway would prove exceedingly difficult to handle. Reinforcements were able to arrive by sea; but in Churchill's view the 'chief limiting factor' from the Allied point of view 'was the provision of the necessary bases and lines of communication on which the forces were to be maintained. The bases would be liable to heavy air attack.'[17] On 19 April the Chiefs of Staff agreed, and both Chamberlain and Churchill concurred, that no direct assault could be made on Trondhjem.[18]

Operations 'Rupert' and 'Maurice' had very different, though interconnected, histories. On 20 April, Namsos was practically obliterated by German bombing. Aandalsnes was also attacked, but the damage was less serious. When the Ministers came to review the position the following day, the first note of alarm was sounded in the War Cabinet. Churchill reported that the situation 'certainly gave rise to some anxiety, but was not by any means desperate'. Oliver Stanley, Secretary for War, considered that 'the French should be told very bluntly what a hazardous operation we were undertaking and how great our difficulties were'.[19]

In the Narvik area, naval operations were controlled by Admiral of the Fleet the Earl of Cork and Orrery, land forces by General Mackesy. As Churchill explained on 21 April,

> It appeared that at one time the Admiral and the General had been agreed on an operation which might be described as a harassing bombardment, to be followed by test landings, but the General had changed his mind after his last reconnaissances. This apparent lack of harmony led the War Office to agree to subordinate the General to the Admiral, who would thus be in supreme command of the whole operation.[20]

Cork asked the War Cabinet whether he could be given permission to bombard Narvik. Churchill was disposed to agree. The Germans, the First Lord suggested, should be given 'say six hours' notice'. Civilian inhabitants would be warned to leave the town. At expiry of the notice, bombardment should commence. Mackesy's objection was on humanitarian grounds:

> He felt it his duty to represent that there was no Officer or man under his Command who would not feel shame for himself and his country if thousands of Norwegians, men, women and children, in Narvik were subject to the proposed bombardment.[21]

This was no egregious squeamishness. Climatic conditions were appalling, and the privations would be extreme.

On one point, however, there was no dispute between the two commanders at Narvik. They needed to know from the War Cabinet whether more troops would be available in the area. This raised in acute form the question which had been simmering ever since the Norwegian campaign was first mooted. It was tacitly accepted that extra troops for 'Rupert' could only be obtained at the cost of 'Maurice'. Churchill had no doubts where priorities should lie:

> Narvik was of vital importance to us, and it was essential that it should be our hands in good time before the ice melted in the Baltic . . .We had therefore only a month in which to liquidate the position at Narvik and it was of the utmost importance not to have our attention diverted by operations elsewhere from our principal objective which had always been from the very start the control of the Gällivare ore-fields.[22]

Stanley was equally emphatic the other way:

> He hoped that we should not now switch our main efforts back on to Narvik. He felt that the correct strategy would be to concentrate our efforts on the operations in Central Norway, and only allot to Narvik the forces which could not be made use of in that area.[23]

Chamberlain seems on the whole to have inclined towards Churchill's view; but a decision was deferred pending a report from Lord Cork.

While all these matters were still unresolved, the Supreme War Council met. Chamberlain's report of its deliberations was enthusiastic. He

> had anticipated considerable difficulties, but the French had given us complete satisfaction and had accepted our views on all points discussed . . . The French were content to leave the strategy of the [Norwegian] operations to us.[24]

The Supreme War Council's advice on the substantive points under discussion, however, was Delphic in its obscurity. The 'capture of Trondhjem was set down as the first objective' – an apparent victory for Stanley and the 'southerners'. However, 'M. Reynaud had made it clear . . . that . . . the main objective was to deprive Germany of her iron ore' – an equally evident victory for Churchill and the 'northerners'. Whether the 'first objective' in one place took priority over the 'main objective' in another was surely a point of theological subtlety.

In the next few days, the balance tilted against the southern expedition. The Germans had seized all important Norwegian airfields at a very early stage of the campaign, and absence of suitable air bases proved crucial. A frozen lake near Aandalsnes was used briefly for fighter aircraft; but almost immediately the Germans bombed it and put out of action sixteen of the eighteen planes based there.[25] The seriousness of the situation was immediately recognised: 'A telegram had stated the importance of sending more fighters to Norway . . . Without this fighter support, it was stated that the Army could not hold out.'[26] If the planes could not be operated even on improvised airfields, the conclusion was inescapable: the southern expedition at least must fail.

The Prime Minister now intervened decisively on Churchill's side in the substantive controversy. Suppose, he argued on 26 April, the Allies even succeeded in their object of seizing Trondhjem. Before it could be used as a base

> it would require about fifty heavy and eighty light anti-aircraft guns . . . Moreover to secure the maintenance of our forces in Norway would require the efforts of the greater part of the Home Fleet, which would be exposed to risks which we should be unwilling to take in view of the possible attitude of Italy. . . . Without Trondhjem there was very little we could do in Central Norway. The division of strength that we should have to make to try and maintain forces ashore would be disproportionate to the ends we sought to achieve.[27]

The Military Co-ordination Committee, reported the Prime Minister, 'had come to the conclusion that plans should be got ready for evacuating our forces from Aandalsnes and Namsos in case of need'.[28]

What removed any doubts from the minds of the War Cabinet was a new military report from the south. On 27 April they were told that the Aandalsnes force might perhaps be evacuated without loss if this was done not later than the night of 1/2 May; but if the operation was delayed beyond that date reinforcements would be necessary to resist the German advance.[29] At Namsos, the problem was almost exactly the reverse: there were too many troops, and they did not have sufficient manoeuvering space.[30]

At first the French were strongly opposed to withdrawal. Reynaud wrote Chamberlain 'such a sharp letter that [he] fully expected serious trouble',[31] and there were urgent discussions with Gamelin. Corbin suggested a new meeting of the Supreme War Council, which was held the following day. Chamberlain recorded that 'differences disappeared when we met and we parted in complete agreement'. Evacuation of the southern expedition took place in the first few days of May. Embarkation was wholly successful, but substantial damage was done by German aircraft to the returning vessels.[32]

Prospects of capturing Narvik were better. When Lord Cork's report on the proposed bombardment was received, the War Cabinet approved Churchill's draft instructions, authorising the Admiral to act as he proposed, provided adequate notice was given.

As Chamberlain was at that moment attending the Supreme War Council, despatch of the telegram was made contingent on his approval.[33] Authority was evidently given, and Cork promptly issued a broadcast warning of the impending action. The bombardment was delayed by bad weather; but when it was eventually begun, a day or two later, results appear to have been only moderately successful.[34]

Grandiose schemes were devised for Narvik's future. 'The plan' – so the British War Cabinet was told on 28 April – 'was to turn Narvik into a miniature Scapa, and already sixty or seventy anti-aircraft guns were available'.[35] Its importance in relation to the iron ore trade had been stated repeatedly. Now – with collapse of the expedition to southern Norway – it acquired further significance: to 'preserve a part of Norway as a seat of Government for the Norwegian King and People'.[36] Perhaps in anticipation of this new function for Narvik, King Haakon was temporarily settled in Tromsø, even further to the north. The Norwegian Parliament, which contrived to meet in Stockholm, adduced a further reason for action against Narvik. On 3 May 'they had decided immediately to telegraph the Norwegian Government recommending that the struggle be continued, but only provided that the Allies did not intend to abandon Narvik and northern Norway'.[37]

Lord Cork found himself between several fires. Allied land forces were certainly pressing on Narvik. As early as 27 April the War Cabinet was told that the town was 'virtually surrounded'.[38] On 4 May, Churchill informed the War Cabinet that Lord Cork proposed 'to seek a decision in the ensuing week' – adding that 'he was wise to do so and . . . his proposed action should be supported whatever the outcome'.[39] A day or so later, however, the Admiral received 'unanimous representations . . . by senior Army Officers to the effect that a direct attack on Narvik in present circumstances would be unjustifiable'.[40] The eventual and astonishing denouement of the Narvik expedition lies outside our story; suffice to say that the town was still invested, but had not yet been assaulted, when the great crisis of the British Government took place a few days later.

A month of spectacular events in Norway somewhat deflected public attention from important happenings which concerned the other northern states. At the beginning of the invasion, it was generally assumed that Sweden would soon be treated in a similar way to her western neighbour. On 10 April, the second day of the

attack on Norway, a series of rather wild rumours suggested that
Germany was mounting enormous pressure, and that the Swedes
'feared that if they refused any demand made by Germany they
would be attacked by the German and Soviet air forces'.[41] Next
day, Halifax recorded a definite opinion: 'it seemed to him most
unlikely that Sweden would succeed in maintaining her neutrality'.[42] The surge of Swedish opinion was embarrassing to the
country's government; a later report told how the news of the
invasions 'aroused the wildest indignation, though official quarters
had imposed the strictest reticence on the Press with regard to
feelings for the countries attacked'.[43]

It was one thing, however, to anticipate that Sweden would soon
be brought into the war, and quite a different thing actively to
encourage her to intervene on the Allied side. In the night of 10/11
April, the British Government learnt that the French had decided to
send a mission to Sweden immediately 'to encourage the Swedes to
maintain a firm attitude against German demands'.[44] The British
Ambassador in Paris felt strongly that any such mission should
include British members, and this view was endorsed by the
Cabinet. Arrangements were swiftly made for the French delegates
to call at London en route, where they were subjected to massive
pressure from Chamberlain, Halifax, Churchill and the three Chiefs
of Staff.[45]

Even before the delegation arrived, its main purpose had really
been fulfilled, for the Swedish Prime Minister had already made a
broadcast speech declaring his Government's intention 'to defend
Swedish liberty against all external and internal enemies'.[46] All
indications were that Sweden would resist German demands for
special facilities, and would fight if attacked – but would not
otherwise go to war. Halifax decided that the general conclusion
was 'quite satisfactory'.[47]

While the British were unwilling to entice Sweden into war by
promises of help which could not be fulfilled, they had no objection
to involving her in war by other means. The original instructions to
General Mackesy at Narvik had been 'that, after landing, he should
push rapidly on to Gällivare'. These orders were soon changed, and
he was instructed to go no further than the Swedish frontier. This
qualification was not inserted out of solicitude for Sweden; as
Churchill told the War Cabinet, 'if Sweden was friendly we should
have no need to be apprehensive about the ore fields, and, if hostile,
the difficulty of pressing on would be too great'.[48]

As the pace of war increased, neither side could afford to be over-scrupulous about the niceties of Swedish neutrality. On 24 April, Hankey submitted to Halifax the argument that it was essential to mine Sweedish territorial waters in order to block German sea-routes into Norway,[49] and the following day the War Cabinet approved this suggestion. A somewhat disquietening qualification was made: 'it was unnecessary to make any notification before the mines had been laid, or to admit that we had laid them'.[50] A few days later, German ship concentrations in Oslo Fjord were interpreted – wrongly, as events proved – 'as indicating the likeli-hood of a German attack upon Sweden'.[51] German pressure, however, was continued, and complaints about Sweden's reactions were heard in the War Cabinet – though not, perhaps, any very serious suggestions of what other options lay open to her. Whatever difference may have existed between the Swedish Government and people at the beginning of the invasions, there was no difference between them as the Allied campaign ground to a halt. Postal censors reported that 'Sweden's strict adherence to neutrality is insisted upon by practically every correspondent in Sweden'.[52]

The Scandinavian invasions produced early and direct reper-cussions in other northern lands. Denmark owned Greenland and the Faroe Islands; while Iceland was an independent state under the Danish king. On the day of the German invasion, the Governor of the Faroes 'agreed to give the necessary facilities to enable British forces to prevent the Germans from establishing themselves in the islands'.[53] A few days later, they were occupied without difficulty. Greenland seemed remote from the European conflict; but the Canadian Government made representations in London that it 'might be desirable for Canadian forces to take action to safeguard the cryolite mines at Ivigut in Greenland, which were of great importance to the Canadian aluminium industry'.[54] The Canadians were assured that there was 'no objection' to this course.

Iceland presented more problems. On the evening of the Scandinavian invasions, the Icelandic Government received a British request for facilities. No early action was taken on either side, but German progress in Norway persuaded the British Government that unless they occupied Iceland soon, the Germans would get there first. Howard Smith, who had been British Minister in Denmark before the invasion, was designated for a similar post in Iceland. On 6 May Halifax advised the War Cabinet that there was no point in asking the Icelanders for concurrence in the occupation, for they 'would inevitably refuse'. The War Cabinet therefore gave its approval for 'the immediate occupation of Iceland by military forces, with a view to the establishment of naval and air facilities'. A couple of days later, four British warships sailed for Reykjavik.[55]

At the moment of the invasions, there appeared a serious possibility that either Italy or Russia – or perhaps even both of them – might be brought into the war on Germany's side in the near future. Indications – such as they were – did not suggest that Japan was proposing to take similar action, at least for the time being.[56]

The Soviet Union might be brought into the war either through her own initiative or through that of the Allies. On the latter point, there was a marked difference between British and French opinion. 'The majority view,' reported the British Ambassador from Paris on 2 April, 'favours the adoption of a more forceful policy towards the U.S.S.R.'[57] The Ambassador went on to add that 'Mr. Churchill's reference in his speech on March 30th, to the undesirability of provoking war with that country was not universally well received'. The French continued to press for expedition in study of the Baku project[58] and at the meeting of the Supreme War Council on 23 April it was again agreed to press ahead with preparations for a possible move in the area – although the Council stipulated that it was designed to meet the situation arising 'if Soviet Russia were to take action against the interests of the Allies.'[59] An investigation with strong backing from Reynaud, and which did not commit anybody to definite military action, could scarcely be resisted. The British view of the whole project, however, was stated in a telegram sent to the Dominions on 20 April:

> We would only embark on hostile actions against the Soviet Union in order to accelerate the defeat of her associate Germany . . . we contemplate that in no case would such a decision be taken unless it was considered an unavoidable necessity in order to bring the war to a swift and victorious close.[60]

Russia showed no sign of any active desire to participate on Germany's side, though she gave little indication of any friendship towards the Allies. An article in *Izvestiya*, just after the Norwegian invasion, '[began] by saying that Allied violation of Norwegian territorial waters compelled Germany to take counter-measures'.[61] Halifax was unwilling to read much into such comments: 'the attitude of Russia was obscure' was the burden of his message to

Ministers the following day.[62] The French remained more suspicious of Soviet intentions. On 15 April Reynaud warned the British Ambassador 'to keep a very watchful eye on Soviet Russia, since he thought it not unlikely that the Germans would offer her Narvik if she liked to come and take it'.[63]

Russia evidently had no intention of taking action which would involve serious risk of war with the Allies, for such small rewards. Furthermore, there were signs that some existing grounds of complaint on both sides might be removed. The Allies objected to the passage of war material from and through Russia to Germany; the Russians objected to Allied contraband control. On 27 March Maisky saw Halifax 'to enquire if we would now be willing to resume our negotiations for a Trade Agreement with the Soviet Government'.[64] The Foreign Secretary was at first very sceptical about the prospects of such an agreement, but felt that 'the possibility of resuming trade negotiations with the Soviet Government should be explored'.[65] The War Cabinet endorsed Halifax's view, and discussions with Russia proceeded – though on a rather low diplomatic key. As time went on, the Foreign Secretary became increasingly convinced that Russia was sincere in her desire to reach agreement.[66] The French throughout were a great deal more dubious than the British about the possibility or desirability of such an agreement; but on 6 May Halifax came to the point of making a conditional recommendation to the Cabinet that Britain should be prepared to enter the trade negotiations Russia desired.[67] By this stage, it is surely correct to say that any danger of war with Russia in the near future had been safely overcome. In a letter to one of the Government's critics, Halifax indicated his own view of Russia's attitude:

It may be true, as you say, that Russia does not want Germany to win, but it is, I fear, equally true that they do not wish the Allies to win either. In short, their game, as I see it, is to do all they can to prolong the war as much as possible in the hope that it will end in a deadlock and general exhaustion, from which they will draw the benefit.[68]

If that analysis was correct, then the more Germany prospered in the war, the more Russia would be likely to lean towards the Allies – and vice versa.

With Italy, the situation was exactly the opposite: the more successful Germany became, the more likely it was that Mussolini would enter the war on Hitler's side. The Italian press, which had taken an attitude so different from the Germans over Finland, enthusiastically supported the German line over Norway. Press reactions in a dictatorship nearly always give an indication of Government attitudes, and this Italian response immediately made people wonder whether Mussolini was trying to 'soften up' Italian opinion in preparation for intervention. A view very commonly stated in diplomatic circles at this time was that

> Signor Mussolini was anxious to enter the war on the German side but was held back by the knowledge that the King and the bulk of the Italian people were against it; none the less, he was sufficiently strong to impose his will on the country in the last resort.[69]

The situation had another aspect, too. It was generally believed that Italy was incapable – for economic reasons if for no others – of waging prolonged war. Mussolini, therefore, would only take Italy into the war if convinced that Germany would win it in the near future.

On 18 March, Hitler and Mussolini met on the Brenner Pass. The usual euphoric public announcements were made, but the real significance of the meeting was speculative. A day or so later, however, rumours emerged from the Balkans. German sources in Greece and Yugoslavia spoke of a possible intention by Italy to attack the Greek island of Corfu.[70] This story was followed by rumours of possible Italian action on the Dalmation coast of Yugoslavia.[71]

Gobbets of information from Vatican suggested that on 12 or 13 April there had been a sharp dispute between Mussolini and his Foreign Minister, Ciano. 'The cause was said to have been Count Ciano's refusal to accept the axiomatic certainty of British defeat.'[72] Thereafter Ciano apparently took to his bed – suffering from influenza, pique, or both. Other snippets of news suggested that on the night of 17/18 April Mussolini met his military advisers, who argued firmly against war; while a day or two later the Duce was reconciled with his son-in-law.[73]

Within a day or two, alarms about Italy returned. A new telegram from the British Minister to the Vatican was reported to the War Cabinet, 'stating that Signor Mussolini had imposed on the

[Fascist] Grand Council his decision to enter the war on or about 1st or 2nd May, and that he would do so by attack on Malta and Gibraltar'.[74] This information was taken sufficiently seriously for Churchill to interfere with proposed naval movements in the Mediterranean.

The speculation about possible Italian action in the Balkans forced diplomats to consider what Britain should do in event of an attack on Greece or Yugoslavia. The engagement to Greece which Britain had undertaken a year earlier left little leeway for mano-euvre there if the Greeks chose to resist; but Yugoslavia was more dubious. Vansittart's advice was emphatic: 'I feel sure that we shall have to go to war with Italy at once, if we possibly can, in the event of an attack on either Yugoslavia or Greece.'[75] The Chiefs of Staff took the same view.[76] Sir Percy Loraine, Ambassador to Rome, was in London at the time and discussed the matter with both Chamberlain and Churchill. 'In both their minds,' he wrote to Halifax, 'there was serious doubt about the advisibility, or the utility for our purposes of beating Germany, of an immediate declaration of war on Italy, and very possible advantage in witholding it.'[77] Fortunately Britain was never faced with the choice; for at the end of April events took another turn, and the emerging view suggested 'that Signor Mussolini no longer con-templated any military initiative'.[78]

Italy was not the only Great Power with aspirations in the Balkan area, and it was likely that any Italian designs had been co-ordinated with Germany and possibly Russia. The innumerable internecine disputes between the Balkan countries, the great practical difficulty of getting Allied help to many parts of the peninsula, and the extreme uncertainty as to from which of three possible quarters aggression would be launched, all operated against the possibility of engineering any kind of useful association between the Balkan countries and the Allies; but did not necessarily inhibit the organisation of a rather ramshackle neutral bloc in the area. A remarkable, and very gloomy, paper on the subject was drawn up by the Foreign Office and circulated to the Cabinet with the apparent approval of Halifax at the end of April. 'Up till now,' the document noted,

we have with a fair amount of success been able to constitute and maintain a front in the Balkans in opposition to German pressure and penetration. Based on Turkey, this front has included

Yugoslavia, Romania, Bulgaria and Greece, with Hungary as a
weakly held outpost. Bulgaria has always been a weak point in
the line, but we have succeeded in recent months in definitely
strengthening our position.

    All this has been accomplished by persistent diplomatic effort
and careful propaganda and nothing much else . . . we have
never been able to reinforce our diplomacy by promises of
military assistance (except in the case of Turkey).[79]

This condition had been maintained through the winter; but, in the
author's view, could not last much longer. 'Hitler had to come
to terms with the Italians and Russians before embarking upon a
Balkan campaign, and this he has probably now done.' No doubt
the three aggressors would each have claims on the peninsula, but
Germany would seize the lion's share: 'It is hardly likely that
[Hitler] will content himself with the acquisition of the Romanian
oil wells . . . His objective would be Constantinople and to a lesser
degree Salonika.' The effect of a German attack was predictable. It

> would bring the whole edifice of Balkan solidarity which we so
> laboriously built up crashing to the ground like a house of cards.
> One or other of the Governments might offer a short resistance,
> but Germany's mastery of the air would enable the German Air
> Force to bomb them into speedy submission, as they bombed
> Poland last September and are now bombing Norway.

When the author asked the crucial question – 'whether there is any
point in South-Eastern Europe where the Allies, in conjunction
with the Turks, can make a stand' – he did not imply that he was
sanguine about the answer.

    Depressing as the picture appeared in southern and south-eastern
Europe, the prospects in the West were even more alarming. The
received view among British military and diplomatic commentators
was that Germany proposed to seek a final decision to the war in
1940. On 4 May, the Chiefs of staff considered two possible ways in
which Germany might attempt to achieve early victory: by an
attack on France or by an attack on Britain. In the former event,
'We estimate that there are at present sufficient land forces to
maintain the security of French territory against both Germany and
Italy if adequate air protection is provided.'[80] The condition, we
now know, was not granted. A more likely direction of German

attack – in the view of the Government's military advisers – was 'by a major offensive against Great Britain'.

Whether Britain or France was to be the main target, Germany's first move would almost certainly be through the Low Countries. Belgium and the Netherlands had already demonstrated their extreme (and embarrassing) anxiety to maintain neutrality. On the day of the Scandinavian invasions, the Supreme War Council resolved 'to send a joint Note to the Belgian Government urging that the Allies should be invited to enter Belgian territory before it was too late'.[81] The Belgians refused – although the Foreign Minister indicated that his Government 'might, however, be prepared to consider our proposal more favourably if they could be assured that the Allied forces would take up a more advanced position'. He went on to add that they 'would, of course, invite us to enter their country the moment they were certain that an attack was imminent'. All this gave scant comfort to the Allies. The Supreme War Council had in fact already decided on 28 March that if the Germans entered Belgium the Allies would march in, with or without invitation.

There remained a further theoretical possibility: that the Germans would invade Holland but not Belgium. This was just conceivable if the ultimate target was Britain to the exclusion of France. The War Cabinet decided on 12 April 'that in the event of a German invasion of Holland the right policy to pursue would be to march into Belgium at once'.[82] This view was eventually adopted by the Supreme War Council, with the explicit rider that intervention should then take place 'without further consultation between the Allied Governments and irrespective of the attitude which the Belgian Government might adopt'.[83]

On 30 April, a report was received from the British Embassy in Rome that the Germans were preparing to attack Belgium and Luxembourg within the next couple of days.[84] That night, Churchill issued orders 'for the action to be taken in the event of a German attack on Belgium or the Netherlands to be held at twelve hours' notice instead of twenty-four'.[85] A few days' grace were given; but in that period the signs of an impending assault became more and more certain. A report came in through Yugoslavia, indicating that vessels were standing by under steam at Hamburg, with the believed objective of seizing the Frisian Islands.[86] The Dutch naval staff, it was soon learned, 'viewed the situation seriously and did not exclude the possibility of a German attack on the islands'.[87] A few days later Halifax reported to his colleagues that Vatican quarters – often a good source of information – 'expected a German invasion in the west to begin that week; according to that information this offensive might include not only the Maginot Line and the Netherlands and Belgium but even Switzerland'.[88]

Thus stood matters in the first week of May 1940. The Allied foothold in Scandinavia was confined to the northern tip of Norway. There was good reason for thinking that the next substantial Allied reverse anywhere would bring Italy into the war on Germany's side. The 'Balkan Front' – such as it was – appeared on the point of collapse in face of Germany, Italy and possibly Russia. Germany was evidently poised to seize the Low Countries, and through them to attack either or both of the Western Allies in hope of an early and decisive victory. The United States, the Soviet Union and Japan stood outside the main conflict, and there was little sign that any of them proposed to intervene. As for the smaller neutrals, the story which we have already recorded from Sweden was typical of many. At one moment, public sentiment had perhaps desired active intervention on the side of the Allies. The awful fate of those who had resisted aggression now disposed Governments and public alike to favour whatever terms they could make with the three predatory dictatorships. As for the Allies, France was clutching wildly at the most harebrained schemes which offered some outside chance of saving her from the full weight of that German attack which daily became more certain. Britain, protected by twenty-two exceedingly useful miles of water, was far more secure; but if she sought not merely to protect herself, but eventually to drive back Germany from her conquests, the prospect of achieving that object must have seemed exceedingly small.

10 Political Crisis

'The most common cry, and this of course is chronic in the U.S.A., is Why are we always too late? Why do we let Hitler take the initiative? Why can't we have the plans which would take him by surprise?

The answer to these questions is simple enough, but the questioners would rather not believe it. It is, Because we are not yet strong enough.' Neville to Hilda Chamberlain, 4 May 1940. NC 18/ 1/1153

At the outbreak of the Second World War, an electoral truce was concluded between the political Parties – as in 1914. While the arrangement lasted, they would not contest by-elections against each other, but would allow vacancies to be filled by the Party which had previously held the seat. The agreement would hold good for the duration of the war – or until any of the three Parties gave notice.[1] An Act of Parliament prescribed that local government elections should not be held during the war, but casual vacancies filled by co-option. Although this was not formally part of the agreement, when 'maverick' Parliamentary candidates appeared, they received no countenance from the central organs of the established Parties. In the early months of the war, Labour had a certain amount of trouble with individual members who supported pacifist or pro-Communist candidates; but the official attitude of the Party was not in doubt. Under the Parliament Act of 1911, a General Election was due not later than the autumn of 1940. In the First World War, Parliament's life had been extended year by year through special legislation; but there was no current understanding that the same thing would apply in the Second. Attlee wrote that it would be 'a dangerous thing to assume . . . that under no circumstances can there be an appeal to the electorate until after the war'.[2]

There was also no very clear understanding about how the Opposition Parties stood on matters which bore on the business of government. As a matter of strict constitutional law, of course, the

Opposition Parties had no right to be consulted at all; but in practice the Government remained in fairly close contact with the Labour Party leaders on matters of foreign policy and defence; though one may argue whether this was a gesture of courtesy or a matter of ordinary prudence.

Opinions of a pacifist or defeatist nature were not unknown in any of the Parties; but there was not the slightest doubt that the official leaderships were wholly committed to the view that the war must be fought to a conclusion, and the vast majority of MPs in all Parties concurred in that opinion. As we have seen, both the Liberal and Labour Parties were unwilling to join the Government at the outset of war. This was partly because of the distrust they entertained for some leading members, and also because they felt that by joining the Administration they would be implicated in its actions, without being able to influence them substantially. In such circumstances, commented Dalton, 'we would not only be uninfluential within, but we should lose most of our power to exert influence from without'.[3]

As time went on, these feelings did not abate; nor did the strong animosity which many people in the Opposition Parties continued to experience towards the Prime Minister. This was not reduced by Chamberlain's unfortunate propensity to see political disagreement in personal terms – a characteristic which shows so clearly in his private correspondence. Even well-informed critics continued to express doubts about Chamberlain's devotion to the war effort, apparently suspecting that he meditated some more spectacular 'Munich'. Those suspicions had no justification; but Chamberlain was not the man to talk informally to people for whom he had little respect, in a manner which might have reassured them on that matter at least. As late as February 1940, Dalton thought it necessary to question Halifax directly on the matter.[4] He went on to tell the Foreign Secretary that Labour were 'much more disinclined to cooperate with [Chamberlain] and some of his colleagues than with certain others, of whom Halifax [was] one'. A month later the future Labour leader Hugh Gaitskell, currently working at the Ministry of Economic Warfare, also needed to assure Dalton that there was no evidence that a desire to 'pack up the war' was entertained by any member of the War Cabinet.[5] If a man as well-informed as Labour's chief spokesman on Foreign Affairs required constant reassurance on such a point, it is not difficult to appreciate the intense suspicion which existed at lower levels of the Labour Party. The Prime Minister's animus against the Liberal leader,

Sinclair, and – *a fortiori* – against Lloyd George, was even stronger than his feeling about the Labour leaders.

In this context, relations between members of the Government itself are also important. In January 1940, Leslie Hore-Belisha, Secretary for War, resigned from the Government. The story is a complex one, and the details need hardly detain us. Chamberlain's orginal intention had been to transfer Hore-Belisha to the Ministry of Information. At a late stage, the Prime Minister discovered that Halifax – probably prompted by Cadogan – was not happy at the proposal, and Hore-Belisha was offered the Board of Trade instead. He regarded this as a mere sop to soften the blow of dismissal[6] and resigned in both distress and pique. The Prime Minister had never intended this result, but both Hore-Belisha and many of the Government's critics believed that he had been sacrificed to placate what were often called 'brass-hats at the War Office'. The new Minister was Oliver Stanley; and from this appointment, too, much trouble would later flow.

Trouble also flowed from the changes introduced at the beginning of April, even though these had initially pleased both Chamberlain and Churchill so much. The new Military Co-ordination Committee did not work smoothly. Churchill, in the Prime Minister's view,

> does enjoy planning a campaign or an operation himself so much and he believes so earnestly in his own ideas (for the moment) that he puts intenser pressure on his staff than he realises. The result is apt to be that they are bullied into a sulky silence – a most dangerous position in war.[7]

The first result here was remarkable. Again we turn to Chamberlain's account:–

> Winston himself fully recognised that he was getting into an impossible position and himself asked me to take the Chair, remarking, 'They'll take from you what they won't take from me.' So I did and held my meetings at 10 each morning. The result was magical. We were always unanimous. Instead of spending hours in arguing over details as I am told the Committee had been doing we finished in about 35 minutes . . . W. C. himself is in the best of humour and tells his friends that he and the P.M. are working admirably together.[8]

Again the euphoria did not last. The Military Co-ordination Committee had another stormy session late one evening, when Chamberlain and Churchill had both just returned from an exhausting day with the Supreme War Council in Paris. After that session, Churchill wrote to the Prime Minister thanking him for 'having at my request taken over' the management of the Committee. Nevertheless, intimated Churchill, 'I shall not be willing to receive the responsibility back from you without the necessary powers'.[9] What were these 'necessary powers'? During a long private talk, Churchill explained what he wanted – 'which was in effect to become Minister of Defence'.[10] Chamberlain attempted to persuade the other two service Ministers, Hoare and Stanley, to give Churchill more or less what he wanted. Their reactions, however, were very sharp:

> They said they would rather he became Defence Minister while they resigned and were succeeded by Under-Secretaries so that everyone should know where responsibility in fact lay. It was only when [Chamberlain] said [he] would rather resign [himself] and let W.C. be Prime Minister as well as Defence Minister that they said that would be too great a disaster and they would do as [he] asked them.[11]

Chamberlain devised an arrangement which seems to have been accepted by all concerned. Churchill's powers were substantially increased, and he 'could not have been more agreeable' when told of the new arrangement. Not even Chamberlain seems to have entertained the view that it would prove more than a stop-gap; but this arrangement seems to have worked smoothly for the week or so of life which remained to the Government.

Thus the position within the Cabinet early in May 1940 was one which would perhaps have astonished both critics and supporters of the Government. Chamberlain stated categorically that 'no decision over Norway has been taken against [Churchill's] advice and although he puts out many nonsensical proposals he very rarely maintains them against reasoned argument'.[12] The most serious disputes within the War Cabinet, both on the machinery of Government and on actions to be taken, had lain between Churchill and Stanley, with Chamberlain doing all in his power to back the former. The irony of the situation is not reduced when one recalls that during the 'Munich' crisis of September 1938, Stanley had been one of Chamberlain's most severe critics within the Cabinet.

In several ways, a situation was building up curiously redolent of that at the beginning of December 1916. Different attitudes to the war certainly did exist in high places; but the two men who were generally recognised as the heads of opposing factions were in little disagreement about the essential policy to be pursued; and – left to themselves without the intervention of putative supporters – could very easily have reached complete agreement on how their respective functions should be devolved. In May 1940, as in December 1916, the course of discussion would have been very different from what it was if the public had had access to vital documents of the time.

When it became apparent to the War Cabinet that Allied troops would soon need to be evacuated from central Norway, it was equally evident that the Government would need to render account of the Norwegian campaign before Parliament and the nation. 'Public opinion', declared Halifax to his colleagues on 28 April,

would demand that two questions should be answered:–
(i) 'Why have we had to evacuate?' . . .
(ii) 'How was it that we got into this position, and why did we not realise what was likely to happen?'[13]

Even if no blame at all had attached to the Government, these two questions would have been difficult to answer. In the first place, there was a great element of disappointment in the Norwegian setback. A very few days before the German attack on Scandinavia, Chamberlain had made a most unfortunate speech in which he proclaimed that Hitler 'has missed the bus'. Churchill had given similar hostages to fortune; for he had told the departing troops that they were 'the vanguard of the armies which we and our French allies will use this summer to purge the soil . . . of Norway from the filthy pollution of Nazi tyranny'. The whole history of the past two years or so gave the man-in-the-street cause to wonder whether there was any point at which the British Government was able to organise even a local defeat upon Germany.

The element of patriotic disappointment was accentuated by security problems inherent in the situation. The public – as we have seen – could not be told that the Trondhjem campaign was to be abandoned until all was ready for evacuation. Thus there was great shock when the news broke. No Minister could stand up and recount the full tale of the involved diplomacy and the innumerable political and economic issues which had been considered in the winter and early spring – that complex and explosive story which bore so intimately on the French, the Russians, the Scandinavians and most of the neutrals. Nor could even the military aspect be discussed properly – not even that part which the Germans must have known. Public opinion was disposed to think that it was weakness in the air which produced the *débâcle* in central Norway. Halifax argued in Cabinet that this was far from the whole story. Maintenance of a land force would have imposed considerable strains on the navy. The effect of that revelation 'might be to create an impression that the Royal Navy was no longer the powerful instrument of war which [the public] had always believed it to be'.[14] Other members of Cabinet were inclined to confute this explanation; but all agreed with the need for caution when the matter was to be discussed in Parliament. The security problem which had been so important at the time of the Trondhjem evacuation was still very much present, and no one expressed the current difficulty better than Churchill:

> It was difficult in any case to have to debate the conduct of the campaign in the House of Commons but it would be almost impossible for the Government adequately to state their case without giving the enemy information as to the reasons for their actions, etc. It would be intolerable that the House of Commons or the Press should make the task of the Government more difficult by insisting on revelations of a kind which would assist the enemy . . .[15]

Thus the Government was compelled, as it were, to fight with one hand tied behind its back; while, meantime, the forces of opposition continued to gather strength. Not only the Labour Party but the Liberals, too, had refused to participate as a Party in the Government at the outbreak of war, and saw no reason to repent of their decision. There were also Government supporters who were disaffected to varying degrees. When Churchill and Eden were taken into the Government in September 1939, Duff Cooper – who had resigned from the Cabinet after Munich – was left outside. L. S. Amery, a Conservative who had held several Cabinet offices in the 1920s, was also omitted. Hore-Belisha felt continuing bitterness about the circumstances of his removal from the War Office. There were various disaffected Ministerial back-benchers, including a body, whose secretary was Robert Boothby, which had made a point of organising private gatherings of Government critics. Clement Davies, chairman of the group, went to the extent of resigning the Government whip in November 1939.

Around the beginning of May 1940, Labour leaders began to cull from various sources – not least from their contacts with French Socialist politicians[16] – a very baleful view of the way in which the Government had handled matters in Scandinavia throughout the previous month, and became disposed to move from passive grumbling to more active criticism. Simultaneously, trouble began to blow up for the Government from a very different quarter, and one far more dangerous to their survival. No one epitomised the view of these new criticis more thoroughly than Admiral of the Fleet Sir Roger Keyes, a Conservative with a distinguished First World War record, who had sat in Parliament since 1931. On 30 April Keyes wrote to Churchill, complaining of 'deplorably pusillani- mous and short-sighted' features in the conduct of the sea war[17] – adding that his opinion was 'pretty prevalent throughout the Fleet'. He was furious about 'the delay in taking offensive action, when Germany first seized several Norwegian ports, before they had time to organise defences', and even at that late date called for 'a smashing Naval blow at Trondhjem, *whatever may happen later*'.

Of course there was no logical unity between these disparate critics, whose antipathy to the Administration was rooted in so many different causes, which had arisen at so many different dates: resentments based on a complex mixture of economic, social, diplomatic, military and personal considerations, wherein the proportions of various ingredients varied infinitely from man to man. By May 1940, however, the overwhelming feeling was that the war was going badly; that radical change was imperative. The critics were in a mood to cheer one another on, without enquiring too closely whether their grounds of criticism were similar, or even compatible.

Until the very end of April 1940, there was no public indication that the Government would soon be fighting for its life. The first salvo was fired on the last day of the month by Sir Archibald Sinclair, who delivered a widely-reported speech in Edinburgh. Even this speech was cautious, although the Liberal leader included the ominous passage: 'If the Government muddles this Norwegian campaign . . . it will be for Parliament to act objectively, fearlessly and resolutely at the grand inquest of the nation'.[18] The *Daily Mail*, traditionally a strong Conservative paper, seized on Sinclair's speech with great avidity, emphasising sharply the more critical passages. On 2 May, the same newspaper reported 'other indications . . . that the Prime Minister will make his statement in a much more critical House than he usually has to face'. The *Daily Mirror* joined eagerly in the same campaign, reading into the Liberal leader's speech an interpretation difficult to draw from its wording: 'Sir Archibald Sinclair is as surprised as we have long been over the surprise of Ministers when the Nazis spring a new surprise on them.'[19] By contrast, the *Daily Herald* was at this stage far more cautious. When it reported Chamberlain's announcement of the Norwegian withdrawal on the following day, Labour's official organ concluded that 'the interim judgment on the Premier's statement yesterday is far from favourable to the Government. In all parties there is disquiet. The Government's prestige has undergone a marked decline'.[20] On 4 May, however, both the *Herald* and the Liberal *News Chronicle* were in full cry against the Government. 'It is now clear that the Government will have to face a very disturbed and critical Parliament,' wrote the *Chronicle*. 'Whoever his fellow-blunderers may be, Mr. Chamberlain has the chief responsibility,' echoed the *Herald*.

At the beginning of the following week, the *Daily Telegraph* was expressing doubts:

> The country has shown that it has no desire or intention to condemn the Government unheard. It awaits the explanation with an open mind, but it will naturally base its judgment on the answers received to various questions which continue to perplex it.[21]

The Times, which spoke strongly for the Prime Minster's ability in Cabinet, was not wholly uncritical: 'What is needed . . . in the public view, is both greater concentration of driving power in the War Cabinet and more time for thinking ahead.'[22] The whole situation puzzled the *Daily Express*, which asked pensively: 'How deep does the Conservative revolt go? . . . It is not serious in the Party itself . . . But in the Conservative newspapers it runs very deep.'[23]

Thus when the great House of Commons debate on the

Norwegian war opened on 7 May 1940, there was everything to show that it would be a major Parliamentary occasion, but a good deal less to indicate that its outcome would decide the fate of the Government. Until the second day of the debate, it was not even clear that the Opposition proposed to divide the House. That morning, however, the Executive of the Parliamentary Labour Party decided, by a majority, to recommend a vote. Dalton and several of his colleagues felt 'that a vote at this stage is likely to consolidate the Government majority and that Chamberlain and Margesson would like to have one'.[24] Later in the morning the body of the Parliamentary Labour Party concurred in its Executive's recommendation – though by no means unanimously.

It was equally uncertain how the Government would respond to Labour's decision to call a vote. One suggestion canvassed in the press and the lobbies was that Chamberlain would promptly announce a General Election – a course of action with some justification since Parliament had only six months to run in the ordinary course of events. In that case, Dalton guessed, 'the Old Man would win hands down and we should be wiped further out than in 1931'.[25]

The tale which the Government had to tell was not one of unrelieved defeat. Great damage – as the Prime Minister pointed out in the debate – had been done to the German fleet. Narvik was still invested, and there was good reason for thinking that it would soon fall. Yet the mood of the House of Commons was profoundly critical. Sir Roger Keyes wore full uniform of his naval rank to emphasise that a large section of Service opinion shared his critical views – and told the House that he had personally offered to lead an assault on Trondhjem. L. S. Amery, who had close political connections with the Chamberlain family, importuned the Prime Minister, in Cromwell's famous words, to 'depart . . . and let us have done with you'. Sir Archibald Sinclair, for the Liberals, declared that 'more foresight and energy, and stronger and more ruthless will to victory, [were] required in the supreme direction of our war effort'. Herbert Morrison, who demanded a division of the House, specifically attacked Chamberlain, Simon and Hoare, indicating his 'genuine apprehension that if these men remain in office we run grave risk of losing the war'. Lloyd George, who for the time being cast from his mind the defeatist thoughts he had entertained a few months earlier, declared the nation's readiness to make sacrifices, and invited the Prime Minister to 'give an example of sacrifice' by surrendering the seals of office.

Neither Chamberlain's unfortunate appeal for support from his 'friends', nor Churchill's spirited defence of the Government's policy, could stem the rising tide of criticism. Whether Members had already made up their minds before the debate; whether they were influenced by what they heard in the chamber; or whether they influenced one another in the lobbies of Parliament – all this is open to conjecture. What is beyond conjecture is the upshot of the debate. The Opposition lobby 'seemed to be full of young Conservatives in uniform'.[26] One of those MPs, A. R. Wise, said later:

> I have come straight back from Namsos to vote against the Government. I voted on behalf of my men. We were bombed by German aeroplanes and had nothing with which to reply, not even a machine gun. When I went back last night to the Mess, everyone, from the Major-General downwards, said 'Well done'.[27]

Whether the Government had acted wisely or not; whether anyone else would have acted better; there was no convincing answer to that kind of criticism.

Technically, the Government won the division by 283 votes to 202. Morally, however, the blow was staggering, for its nominal majority was over 200. Forty MPs who had originally been returned as Government supporters went into the lobbies against it. The quality of the Ministerial rebels was even more impressive than their quantity. Five Privy Councillors who normally took the Government whip voted against it. With them went predictable rebels like Harold Macmillan, Richard Law and General Spears; but so also went Quintin Hogg, whose successful defence of Oxford City at the first by-election after Munich had infused heart into the National Government. *The Times* reported a further sixty-five Conservative MPs 'absent unpaired'; how many of these deliberately abstained we may never know.[28]

The whole press now accepted the need for drastic Government changes. 'The Parliamentary vote on the Norway debate was virtually a Government defeat,' wrote the *Daily Mail*. 'It is urgent that Mr. Chamberlain should undertake the reorganisation of the Cabinet without delay,' declared the *Daily Telegraph*. 'The re-organisation will necessarily be deep and sweeping,' concurred the

Daily Express. 'Out of the evil of the Norwegian fiasco at least one good thing has come,' observed the *Evening News*: 'It is the certainty of a new Government.' *The Times* took the opposite view of Labour's decision to press matters to a vote: 'From the public standpoint it was a great misfortune': but did not dissent from the substantive conclusion that changes of a radical nature were necessary.[29]

Chamberlain was not without his supporters. Lord Rothermere, for many years proprietor of the *Daily Mail*, telegraphed, 'Entirely disapprove *Daily Mail* attitude regarding Government. I have nothing whatever to do with paper. My remonstrances passed unheeded.'[30] Robert Menzies, Prime Minister of Australia, was deeply upset: 'Hysteria and search for a scapegoat are I suppose inevitable in time of war but they have left me very sick at heart.'[31]

In a broadcast two days after the critical division, Chamberlain indicated his own reactions:

> When it was over I had no doubt in my mind that some new and drastic action must be taken if confidence was to be restored to the House of Commons and the war carried on with the energy and vigour essential to victory . . . It was clear that . . . what was needed was the formation of a Government which would include members of the Labour and Liberal Oppositions and thus present a united front to the enemy.

To that extent, the Government's miscellaneous critics would have agreed with the Prime Minister. Everybody desired a broad Coalition. Nobody thought, for example, of attempting to drive all the Ministers on to the Opposition benches, and forming an administration from the Government's critics. Everybody wanted Halifax and Churchill to remain in the new Coalition. The real controversy centred on the position of three men: Chamberlain, Simon and Hoare, who were seen by a large section of the Labour Party as a sort of demonic trinity.

Even before the critical division of 8 May, Dalton had discussed with R. A. Butler the possible character of a remodelled Government. He observed that he was not authorised to speak on behalf of his colleagues, but that, in his view,

> provided Chamberlain, Simon and Hoare disappeared from the Government altogether, we should be prepared to discuss the

question of entering the Government . . . I added that, if I was
asked who should succeed Chamberlain as Prime Minister, my
own view, which I thought was shared by a number of others, was
that it should be Halifax.[32]

Butler's account of the interview suggested that Labour's preference
for Halifax was even more emphatic. 'Dalton', he wrote to the
Foreign Secretary, 'said there was no other choice but you.
Churchill must "stick to the war".'[33] This view may seem
anomalous, for Halifax was a peer, and also shared full Ministerial
responsibility for those policies of which Labour had been so critical
over so long a period. One suspects an element of craft. With a
Prime Minister who was a Conservative, and who sat in the Lords,
the chief Government spokesman in the Commons would almost
inevitably be a Labour man. The doubts felt by the Labour Party at
that arrangement seem to have been rooted much more in a feeling
that Attlee was inadequate for the second post than that Halifax was
inadequate for the first.[34] The possibility that a Labour member
might occupy the Premiership was barely discussed. Lloyd George
did mention the possibility that if Chamberlain resigned the King
might call for Attlee; but the Labour leader seemed to accept the
view that the Prime Minister must be a Conservative.[35] Lloyd
George's own name was canvassed briefly by the *Daily Mail*,[36] but
the suggestion was not widely taken up.

Either Chamberlain had not wholly given up hope of remaining
Prime Minister himself, or he was concerned to prove to his keenest
supporters beyond all doubt that a change was politically imperative. In the evening of 9 May he invited Attlee and Greenwood to
serve under him in a remodelled Ministry:

> They . . . told him bluntly that this was impossible and that the
> mood of the country required a new premiership. He then asked
> would they serve under a new Premier. They said they could give
> no answer to this before consulting colleagues.[37]

This statement was hardly an adequate reply, and Chamberlain
asked them for an early and definite answer.

Next day, everything happened together in a rush. Very early in
the morning came news of the German invasion of the Netherlands
and Belgium. Nobody doubted that the new German aggression
was prelude to a major assault on one or both of the Western

Democracies. The question of establishing a strong and stable Government in Britain, which would carry almost universal support, thus acquired a high measure of urgency.

That morning, 10 May, the annual conference of the Labour Party was due to open at Bournemouth. Labour's National Executive Committee met in the afternoon to discuss the Party's attitude to the proposal that it should enter a new Government. At last an authoritative (and unanimous) statement on the subject was issued. Labour was 'prepared to take its share of responsibility as a full partner in a new Government under a new Prime Minister which would command the confidence of the nation'.[38] Attlee and Greenwood were charged to go to London to carry on the necessary negotiations. Labour did not insist – as Dalton had thought they would – that their three particular enemies should be dropped altogether from the Government – merely that Chamberlain should cease to be Prime Minister.

At 4.30 p.m., the Cabinet met. News of the Labour Party's decision had just been received. Chamberlain 'said that, in the light of this answer, he had reached the conclusion that the right course was that he should at once tender his resignation to the King. He proposed to do so that evening'.[39] His colleagues placed their resignations at his disposal.

Like the Labour Party, Chamberlain had orginally favoured Halifax as a successor. The Foreign Secretary – as the Prime Minister reported

> declared . . . that after careful reflection he would find it too difficult, being in the Lords, whereas trouble always arose in the Commons. Later I heard that the Labour Party had changed their minds and were moving towards Winston and I agreed with him and Halifax that I would put Winston's name to the King.[40]

In the early evening of 10 May 1940, Winston Churchill became Prime Minister.

The new Ministry was announced in several stages over the next few days. It centred on a War Cabinet of only five members. Churchill combined with his first office the post of Minister of Defence. Halifax retained the Foreign Office. Chamberlain was first offered his old post of the Exchequer, but 'saw it was impossible, with Labour's set at me'.[41] Instead he became Lord President of the

Council: a virtually non-Departmental function, which carried a seat in the War Cabinet. Attlee and Greenwood both also entered the War Cabinet with non-Departmental duties.

Two members of the old War Cabinet – Hoare and Stanley – were dropped from the Government altogether, while Wood, Hankey and Simon all received Ministerial posts outside the War Cabinet. Of the Liberals, Sinclair became Secretary of State for Air, but – to the surprise of some commentators – was not included in the War Cabinet. One possible reason for this exclusion was that if one service Minister had been included it would have been impossible to resist the claims of the others; and Churchill's great concern was to retain complete control of the war effort. Lloyd George was omitted from the Government. This also occasioned some comment, and seemed to admit of several possible interpretations. The junior offices of government were allocated between the three Parties in proportions appropriate to a true Coalition.

Thus did Churchill find himself in a position in some ways similar to that of Lloyd George in the earlier war; but in others immeasurably stronger. With the doubtful exception of Lloyd George himself, there was nobody outside the Ministry who could possibly be seen as an 'alternative Prime Minister'. With the few exceptions we have noted, everyone received more or less that rank to which his status and the size of his Party would seem to entitle him. Thus Churchill acquired a degree of political security which Lloyd George never had. A few days later, Churchill sought a Vote of Confidence from the House of Commons for his administration and its policy towards the war. The two ILP members present challenged a division, and told in the 'No' lobby. They received no single supporter; for the lone Communist who might have voted with them was for some obscure reason unaware that the House would be meeting.[42]

What, we may now ask, was the reason for the enormous contrast between these two Parliamentary votes: the moral defeat of Chamberlain on 8 May, and the practically unanimous support for Churchill five days later? Hardly the personnel of the two Governments. Few people could confute the view that Churchill was better fitted than Chamberlain to direct a great war; but he had already acquired direction of that war before the old Government fell. The departures of those few senior Ministers who were dropped from the Government scarcely made a radical change in its character.

Did the difference, then, lie in the calibre of the new men who entered the Government? A few days earlier an unkind newspaper columnist had made scathing, but valid, remarks about Attlee: 'Why, it was only a few short months ago that the Socialists were seriously discussing his deposition from the leadership of the Labour Party on the grounds that he lacked energy and initiative.'[43] As for the other man who now joined the War Cabinet, there is little reason to dissent from Chamberlain's judgement: 'Although Greenwood would be amiable and agreeable enough I do not think he could contribute much else.'[44] Sinclair, by contrast, was considerably more charismatic. He was an impressive orator and universally admired in his Party. He had served, though briefly, in Cabinet, and Churchill had already given abundant evidence of the high regard he held for the Liberal leader's ability. Yet Sinclair, as we have seen, was not included in the War Cabinet. Nor where the two Labour men who had given most abundant evidence of their capacity. Herbert Morrison had proved his administrative skill as an outstanding leader of the London County Council; Ernest Bevin had shown his as one of the greatest trade union leaders of the age. Morrison's comment in the privacy of the Labour Party's National Executive was pertinent, though perhaps influenced by 'sour grapes': 'this didn't sound like a Government that would stand up any better than the last one'.[45] The new appointments had been made essentially for the political reason of ensuring that the Government commanded maximum support from Parliament, press and public, and not because any informed observer believed that the people concerned possessed exceptional capacity in the conduct of war. Yet what matters in life is not so much what has happened as what people think has happened; and for that reason the changes were probably justified. Not many people, even of Chamberlain's strongest partisans, were deeply aggrieved, and a great many people saw them as evidence of a new and overriding determination to win the war.

11 Retrospect

ἀμυνῶ δ᾽, ὅσονπερ δυνατός εἰμι, τῷ νόμῳ, τὸ θηριῶδες τοῦτο καὶ
μιαιφόνον παύων, ὅ καὶ γῆν καὶ πόλεις ὅλλυσ᾽ ἀεί.

'So long as I am able, I resist by the law that beastly and murderous
thing which destroys both the land and cities.' Euripides, *Orestes*,
523–5

Historians are forced to seize upon particular events in order to
divide their 'periods' from each other. Some of these events
represent real turning-points in human affairs; but the majority are
no more than convenient 'markers'. The two events which have
been chosen to signal the beginning and the end of this narrative are
of the second kind. The seizure of Prague in March 1939 marked the
formal demise of 'Appeasement'; but Appeasement had been in
poor and rapidly declining health for several months. The for-
mation of Winston Churchill's Government in May 1940 is also to a
large extent an artificial 'marker'. The shift of power from
Chamberlain to Churchill had been gradual and continuous for
eight months already; and Chamberlain remained an important
member of the Government for nearly five months more, until he
was almost on the edge of the grave. The incomers to the
Government from other Parties did not give the new Administration a significantly more robust appearance than its predecessor;
although they undeniably conferred political stability. The change
of character in the war itself is more significant, although in a sense
even this was a mere continuation of the 'hotting-up' process which
had been developing for many weeks.

The real value of mid-May 1940 as a historical 'marker' is that it
becomes possible at that point to discern a new stage in the
development of the public mind in Britain. 'Public opinion' is
difficult to define, and even more difficult to test; but available
indications suggest that those doubts and qualms about the war

itself which had beset many people in late 1939 were largely stilled. Not least significant was the response of nearly all the Government's critics to the bad news from the Norwegian expedition. It was anger – no doubt often ill-informed or misplaced anger, but anger none the less. Apart from the Communists, who were doing all in their power to sap the nation's fighting spirit, these angry people – whatever their differences – concurred in one thing: that the war must be waged more intensely in the future. Just as March 1939 was the first moment when one could say with certainty that Appeasement was dead, so also was May 1940 the first moment when one could say with certainty that the nation was almost unanimous in its determination to wage war, and prepared to pay whatever cost might be demanded.

The demise of Appeasement had not been followed by the emergence of any policy which seemed to offer better prospects of dealing with Hitler. The 'Grand Alliance' so confidently proposed as an alternative neither halted the drift to war nor checked Hitler. By the spring of 1940 it was evident that nobody was likely to join the Allies unless Germany actually attacked them.

Many people had long argued that Appeasement was the product of mere wishful thinking, in the teeth of the evidence. Perhaps this was correct; but so also was the alternative policy begotten of wishful thinking. With the occupation of Prague, most Britons currently saw Nazi Germany as a man-eating tiger which must be caged or destroyed, for otherwise nobody was safe. It was tacitly assumed that matters looked the same to most other countries; that, with the possible exceptions of Italy, Japan and Spain, every other significant nation devoutly desired the containment of Germany, and would render at least passive sympathy and perhaps active support, once a clear lead was given by Britain and France.

Unfortunately, in an extremely dangerous world, there was more than one man-eating tiger on the rampage. The tiger which seemed most dangerous to Britain and France did not necessarily seem the most dangerous to other people – even to people who lived under systems of Parliamentary democracy. To Finland the threat from Russia was far closer. At one moment early in 1940, Sweden had almost equally good reason to anticipate attack from Russia, from Germany and from the Western Allies themselves. The assailant which Greece feared was Italy. The Poles had equal reasons for apprehensions about Russia and Germany. The Romanians shared those two fears; but they were also concerned about the possible designs of Hungary and Bulgaria. In their overwhelming concern with Germany, the Allies did not always show full appreciation of the way in which matters looked from other quarters.

The United States was the one large country which did, on the whole, fit in with the British model of how a neutral ought to think about the war. Yet even the United States did not fully match up to expectations when it came to positive action. There was little doubt that the vast majority of Americans desired an Allied victory, and many of them perceived that an over-mighty Germany could prove a threat to themselves. Congress's amendment of the Neutrality Act in November 1939 was of great value to the Allies; for it permitted them to obtain arms from across the Atlantic; but a couple of months later Britain ran into serious American criticism for the way in which she employed belligerent rights against American shipping. The visit to Europe of President Roosevelt's personal emissary, Sumner Welles, raised again the embarrassing idea of some kind of compromise peace; and the Allies were set in some difficulty when they attempted the phrase a refusal in terms which would not antagonise United States opinion. This particular problem was soon overcome, for the German invasion of Norway and Denmark greatly shocked the Americans; but there was not the slightest indication that they would intervene to the point of war on the Allied side unless the German menace to themselves became much more direct.

If that was how matters stood with the United States, most European countries were a good deal less enthusiastic for the Allies. A cameo, as it were, of one kind of 'neutral problem' was provided by Sweden. In the First World War, she had tended to sympathise with Germany – not because she preferred Germany to the Western Allies, but because she preferred Germany to Russia. Finland in those days was subject to the Tsar; in Finland lived many people of Swedish race and language. The coming of revolution in Russia did not make that country any more attractive to the Swedes. 'Now the Bolsheviks were on the march,' declared King Gustav in December 1939, 'and would be the only victors if the war continued.'[1] When Winston Churchill, obsessed with the danger from Germany, made a speech in which he argued that Russia's increasing activity was probably designed to safeguard herself against that threat, the effect in Sweden was exactly the opposite of what he intended.[2] To many Swedes – as good democrats as any in the world – it was impossible to look without a measure of favour at a Power which might conceivably curtail the Russian menace to themselves. British propaganda in Sweden would have been a good deal more successful if it had emphasised the closeness of the Russo-German alliance.

The Western Allies encountered other difficulties in handling neutral countries. On occasions, it was clear enough to some neutral that the immediate threat came from Germany, and the Western Allies were anxious to persuade that country to resist the Nazi threat. It was natural enough for the neutral to reply, 'If we do so, and Hitler invades us, how much help will you give?' This was more than a paraphrase of the question, 'Will you win the war or will Germany?' If Germany won the war, no one had much doubt that those who had stood in her path would suffer grievously. Yet even if Germany lost, the short-term consequences of German invasion would be appalling. In a matter of this kind, interests of 'grand strategy' might well cut across the immediate needs of potential allies. This was well shown in the Norwegian campaign. To the Norwegians themselves, Trondhjem was far more important than Narvik. From the point of view of the Western Allies, however, Narvik was probably the easier to capture, and certainly the easier to hold thereafter; furthermore, it was much more important in their 'grand strategy'.

The problem of Belgium highlights another aspect of the Allies' difficulties. They had some hope of defending the country against German attack, and its preservation was important to their 'grand strategy'. Everyone recalled the heroic stand of King Albert in 1914, and the victory which eventually crowned that heroism. Yet the immediate effect for Belgium had been a period of four years in which most of the country was occupied by hostile troops, and the remainder was a battlefield. A patriotic Belgian could reasonably ask whether his country would have fared better if King Albert had been less heroic, and the Germans had been permitted to enter with no more than a formal protest. Such reflections on the past no doubt influenced Belgium's current attitude at the beginning of 1940. There was much reason for thinking that the Germans would soon invade the country. If the Allies were permitted to enter Belgium before this happened, the prospects of maintaining a successful defence were a good deal brighter than if Germany was allowed to choose her own moment. Yet Belgium persisted in refusing that permission, and the Allies were never quite certain that Belgium would defend herself if the attack came. When the invasion did occur, Belgium was discovered not merely to lack any common defence plan with the Allies, but not even to have organised mutual defence with the Netherlands.

The difficulties which the Allies encountered in rallying neutrals to their banner were not reduced by the stark contrast between the fate of those who resisted Germany and those who did not. The experience of Denmark or even Czechoslovakia was a great deal milder than that of the much more heroic Poland. A citizen in a small neutral country could perhaps reflect that involvement of his own country in active hostility against Germany would add little to the prospects of eventual Allied victory, but would bring condign punishment upon his own land. British statesmen and diplomats did not always show much understanding – still less sympathy – for those who took this view.

If the Allies failed to win the active support of neutral countries, their necessary belligerent activities frequently reduced even passive sympathy: a problem we have already noted in connection with the United States. The strongest military weapon the Allies possessed at the beginning was their power to organise blockades. Unfortunately, this meant interfering with the interests of neutrals. Their trade would be lost, their ships sunk. War trade agreements were concluded with various countries; but as soon as the blockade began to bite, it was inevitable that ill-feeling would be engendered – not only in the country directly affected, but in other neutrals as well. We have already noted the furious protest which Norway lodged against the minelaying which was no more than a logical extension of blockade; and it may not be fanciful to perceive some connection between current Norwegian feeling against Britain just before the German invasion and the poor showing which Norway made in her own defence when that invasion came.

Churchill in particular made valiant efforts to explain to neutrals that their ultimate interests lay in an Allied victory. Exigencies of war, he argued, might sometimes force the Allies temporarily to infringe those interests; but neutrals would recover full independence and freedom if the Allies won, while they would be dominated by the Nazis if Germany won. This was certainly Britain's intention; but it did not dull the anger of people who only perceived that it was the Allies who were currently doing them injury.

Through these various means were the prospects of a 'Grand

Alliance' dispelled. Long before May 1940, Britain and France were hardly seeing themselves as the centre of a future confederation which would push back the frontiers of Germany; they were fighting with decreasing prospects of success for their own survival.

The closing months of peace and the beginning of war saw the end of another illusion – one not wholly unrelated to the 'Grand Alliance' theory. This was the view which insisted on seeing ideological differences as the determinants of political action. This 'ideological' view was one which particularly ensnared 'intellectuals', who insisted on seeing most international issues in terms of attitudes to fascism or to communism; to socialism or to capitalism; to parliamentary democracy or to totalitarianism.

People who believed that the ideological similarities between Germany and Italy made them inevitable allies in war would naturally urge that they should be treated accordingly. This hindered Governments which sought a timely accommodation with Italy. Scathing things were written about Italy in newspapers, which fed Mussolini's conviction that the Allies were his implacable enemies and Hitler his only friend. Similar considerations applied in attitudes to Russia. Because people favoured, or opposed, the economic and political system in the Soviet Union, they insisted on interpreting the international designs of the country in a favourable or a hostile light. The part played by ideologically motivated journalists in the genesis of the Second World War – and in adding to the Allies' difficulties once it had started – may have been very considerable.

To diplomats and to the man-in-the-street alike, the issues of international politics were seen in completely different terms. It would be quite easy to write a history of European diplomacy in our present period without mentioning any 'ideological' words like fascism, communism or democracy from start to finish. Ideology was something which could be invoked or suppressed at will, according to whether it supported or ran counter to 'national interests' as perceived in terms of classical *Realpolitik*.

Thus the foreign policy of a country often showed a continuity which overrode the most dramatic political changes. Russia, in the nineteenth century, had invoked 'Pan-Slavism', or her self-appointed role as protector of the Eastern Christians, when it suited her purpose; but quietly forgot those 'ideologies' the moment they ceased to be of use to her. Russia employed communism in exactly the same way in the middle third of the twentieth century. If it suited Russia's perceived interests to ally with the Western Democracies in order to preserve the European *status quo*, then communist parties and communist ideology would be exploited to the full in order to engineer such an alliance. If Russia came to consider that it was in her interest to tolerate or even to encourage German aggression, then those same instruments would be used to sap the will of Britain and – far more so – of France to combat Germany. If Russia thought that she had a chance of toppling the Finnish Government through internal subversion, she would conjure up Kuusinen; if she came to decide that no such prospect existed, and the game of completely crushing Finland by force of arms was not worth the candle, then Russia would allow Kuusinen to vanish from the scene.

All of this proved exceedingly tiresome for the ideologists. The communist ideologist had to explain why it was an appalling sin for the Western Allies to appease Germany in 1938, and an equally appalling sin for them to fight her in 1939. The democratic ideologist, who until August 1939 had tried to persuade himself that Stalin was a democrat at heart, was relieved for a short space from that particular difficulty; although the problem would return with a vengeance in 1941.

The vagaries of Russian behaviour were the subject of particular comment, and often of soul-searching, because of the intense sympathy and antipathy which were roused by the political and economic system prevailing in the Soviet Union, and because people who saw international affairs in ideological terms insisted that Russia's behaviour must be either egregiously virtuous or egregiously evil. Yet the paradoxes of Russia's actions from this standpoint differ only in degree from the paradoxes which faced the ideologist in interpreting the behaviour of other states. Britain and France were commonly seen as exponents of Parliamentary democracy. This did not deter them from attempting to ally with eastern countries which were emphatically not democracies; nor did they have great qualms about bullying northern democracies when this seemed expedient. In the summer of 1939, France was willing to contemplate the most astonishing infringments of the interests of democratic Finland, provided those actions would bring the most thoroughgoing totalitarian state in the world into alliance against Germany; yet, six months later, France was equally willing to make war on Russia in ostensible defence of Finland. Even Britain was prepared to incur serious risks of war against Norway and Sweden. It was the merest chance of geography and military strategy which determined that Norway should eventually stand on the Allied side, Sweden should be neutral throughout the war, and – after 1941 – Finland should fight on the side of the Germans.

The vagaries of German behaviour were equally difficult to square with Nazi ideology. One of the most fundamental features of Nazi theory was the conflict between Teuton and Slav, which was seen in racial as well as economic or political terms. Yet Germany suffered the small and helpless Slovak state – undeniably Slav – to survive in comparative quiet throughout the period that Hitler dominated Europe. At a later stage of the war, she evinced a similar toleration towards Croatia. On another interpretation of Nazi 'ideology' the great enemy was 'bolshevism'. This did not deter Germany from making an alliance with Russia, which was both bolshevik and Slav. Nor did Hitler allow his almost equally vigorous prejudices against 'decadent Latins' to vitiate relations with Mussolini. He was not disposed, for example, to press the claims of South Tyrol Germans in a manner which might antagonise the Duce. Hitler was even glad to exploit the grievances of Semitic Arabs to weaken the position of Teutonic Anglo-Saxons in the Levant.

It would not be difficult to find similar paradoxes and contradictions in the behaviour of any other state. Nobody behaved in a manner rooted in ideology, when that ideology ran counter to perceived immediate interests. Hitler's *Mein Kampf*; Stalin's *Problems of Leninism*; or a libertarian declaration like Mill's *On Liberty;* all such works might be brought down from their shelves and dusted when it seemed expedient to do so; but they were quickly replaced, or given twisted 'interpretations', the moment 'national interest' demanded some course of action inconsistent with these precepts.

If we are driven away from an ideological interpretation of events to a *Realpolitik* view of 'national interests', it is necessary to ask what were perceived to be 'national interests'. The Marxist view that these were the interests of the 'ruling classes' is demonstrably wrong. In Britain, in France, and in Germany, the economically powerful groups – the 'ruling classes' – were far more pacifist than the poorer classes. In Britain, most Conservatives supported Appeasement in 1938, and Socialists on the whole opposed it. In France – at least down to the Russo-German Pact – those who favoured armed resistance to Germany were more prominent on the 'left' than on the 'right'. Evidence from Germany suggests that wealthier and older people were appalled at the risks entailed by Hitler's actions; while the poorer and younger people were delighted by everything he did. Indeed, many grievous misinterpretations of German designs, and of likely German behaviour in event of war, were rooted in the fact that so many of the Germans with whom British diplomatic and Government circles had contact were wealthy people who viewed the Nazis with much distaste. The reason for the relative pacifism of 'ruling classes' is not difficult to seek; for they were people who had everything to lose by international disruption. If the 'ruling classes' had had matters their way, we may be absolutely certain there would have been no 1939 war. Yet in all three countries they were either overridden, or belatedly converted, by people in lower social and economic groups who saw the 'nation' in corporate terms, and were prepared to sacrifice everything to it.

Yet 'national interests' were not seen simply in terms of the likely benefit which would accrue from one or another possible course of action. Although Lord Chatfield had argued, early in 1937, that German designs in the east might ultimately run against British interests,[3] and although Vansittart and others pointed out again and again the long-term dangers to Britain from an over-mighty Germany, it is doubtful whether such reasoning ultimately determined the course of British policy. There was not much attempt to cost the advantages and disadvantages of various possible courses of international action, whether in human or in economic terms. The 'gut feeling' at all levels of British society during the last few months of peace was that Germany must be resisted to the point of war, whatever the consequences. In that sense the guarantee to Poland was neither prudent nor imprudent but inevitable. No British Government could at that moment have avoided serving a notice upon Germany that her next major move would constitute a *casus belli*.

By the end of March 1939, it was therefore a strong probability that Britain, France and Poland would soon be fighting as allies against Germany. What seems most astonishing of all was the total failure of the three Allies to co-ordinate plans for that event. The British Cabinet was in doubt as far back as May 1939 whether France would launch any serious diversionary attack in the West if Germany invaded Poland. Once war had been actually declared, the new War Cabinet had to discover again that Gamelin had no such plans – or, if he had any plans, he had no intention of revealing them to anybody (including, one suspects, the French Government itself).

If the Western Allies had failed to co-ordinate strategy with one another, they had failed even more abjectly to devise a common plan with Poland. Whether the British had the capacity to launch an offensive by air, or the French an attack by land, which would have made any substantial difference to the situation, is open to great doubt; but it might have been of some use to Poland to know how much, or how little, succour she could expect.

The Polish war was no more than a gesture. The Polish leaders very likely perceived from the start that – barring revolution in Germany – they had no hope of sustained defence. Their object was apparently to lay claim for restoration of Poland after the war, not to preserve it against the immediate assault. As for the Western Allies, they seem to have lost all sight of the original object of an eastern alliance, which had been to present Germany with a two-front war. Polish resistance was not conceived as a strategic, but as a diplomatic, requirement.

Perhaps, however, we are trying to read more into the situation than the evidence will allow. There is singularly little to show that people had thought through the likely course of events, however crudely and inaccurately. All three Allied Governments were really the prisoners of opinion within their own countries. No Polish Government could concede a square inch of Polish territory, for all Poles knew only too well the history of the eighteenth-century partitions. No British Government could refuse to declare war when next Germany advanced against her neighbours. The extra-ordinary story of the House of Commons revolt on 2 September 1939, when some MPs wrongly thought that the Government was trying to escape its obligations, is clear enough proof of that. No French Government could default on its Polish treaty, for to do so would be to admit that France was no longer a Great Power.

To say that public opinion in the Allied countries would have forced the hand of their Governments, whatever those Governments had tried to do, is one thing; to say that public opinion was wise is very different. In Britain, which is the subject of our present study, there was a tacit assumption running through all political Parties and practically all shades of opinion within those Parties, to the effect that it lay within the power of a British Government radically to affect the political and military situation on the Continent. That assumption was proved completely false within a very few weeks of the end of the period we have studied. It was thoroughly reasonable for Churchill then to proclaim, 'We will never surrender'. The object for which Britain took up arms, however, was not to resist surrendering herself, but to compel Germany to surrender some at least of her conquests, and to renounce a Government whose international word was worthless. This Britain was in no position to do. The task of compelling Germany to surrender was one in which Britain would play a most honourable part; but the sheer weight of numbers and machines required must necessarily come principally from others.

A powerful argument thus exists for the view that the commitment which Britain undertook to Poland, and the much earlier commitment to France, were both disastrous from the point of view of all three countries. Nobody could save Poland from destruction once the war came. In a perverse way, the Polish High Command performed a great service to its country by its sheer incompetence; for this shortened the agony of Poland's hopeless struggle. Poland, perhaps, had no alternative but to resist the German invasion; yet any reliance she may have placed on the Western Allies did her no good in either the short or the long run. A greater proportion of her people than of any other nation died in the war; half of pre-war Poland now belongs to the Soviet Union; and no part of the country enjoys much freedom to this day.

Nor did either Britain or France benefit from the alliance. Britain encouraged France to fight when her heart was not in it. France successfully baulked at the brink of war in September 1938; she attempted the same without success a year later. Thereafter she refused to launch war in Western Europe where it might provoke a German retaliation upon herself, but did everything in her power to prod Britain into war elsewhere, where others would stand the main impact rather than France. Thus was Britain brought into the Norwegian fiasco, and very nearly driven into an incomparably more dangerous involvement with Russia.

The underlying principle of Bonnet's pusillanimity and Reynaud's foolhardiness was the same: to keep the Germans from ravaging France. The same principle led with equal logic from the policy of Reynaud to that of Pétain. The French could complain that their British allies prevented them from getting much better terms from Germany much earlier; that there was no 'equality of sacrifice' between the two Western Allies. The British could complain with equal validity that it was their concern to preserve

France's status as a Great Power which compelled them to underwrite France's eastern alliances, which had been undertaken against British advice in 1925. The two countries really had such utterly different interests that any mutual commitment between them was bound to lead to infinite recriminations, and little positive benefit to either. Britain could not save France from destruction in mid-1940; France could not contribute thereafter to the preservation of Britain.

We have said that it was the condition of British public opinion which made participation in the Second World War inevitable. What, we may ask, so profoundly shocked that opinion? Perhaps different things with different people. Some were angered at the fact of German aggression against neighbouring countries, and were determined that Hitler should never 'get away with it' again. Some were sickened at the atrocities of the Nazis against individuals. Yet no major nation had a history free from the record of aggression, and Hitler had no monopoly of acts of inhumanity.

There was one feature of Nazism which perhaps overrode all others in the minds of statesmen and diplomats: which made any real understanding with Germany impossible after March 1939, and caused British Ministers to reject almost out of hand any argument for peace negotiations once war had been declared. This was the completely unreliable nature of Hitler's word. On the assumption that Britain proposed to intervene in the affairs of Europe at all, this fact alone made it inevitable that she should intervene to the point of war against Nazi Germany. 'The point on which I am in disagreement with you,' wrote Chamberlain to one advocate of peace negotiations at the beginning of 1940,

> is that I do not believe that until Germany gives proof of a change of heart a negotiated peace would be a lasting peace or provide us with those stable conditions which we all so earnestly desire.[4]

Whatever doubts there might be about any other 'war aims', it was clear that no kind of settlement could be concluded while Hitler remained in office. The trouble was not so much that Hitler would drive a hard bargain as that all his bargains were worthless. The one absolutely certain 'war aim' at this stage of the war was the establishment of a Government in Germany which seemed likely to keep its word.

This seems at first sight almost a legalistic issue on which to imperil millions of human lives; yet, when we reflect, we see the force of Chamberlain's answer. In the affairs of human individuals, no society can last unless men are prepared to accept certain relationships with one another. In primitive societies such relations are defined mainly by status; in more advanced societies largely by contract. If it becomes the fashion to deny these relationships – as has happened in some social revolutions – then the whole society dissolves in chaos.

The international issue was similar. Hitler's violation of the Munich agreement in March 1939 was far more than the invasion of a small country and the establishment of a tyrannical regime upon unwilling subjects. It served as plain notice that Nazi Germany proposed henceforth to disregard all international undertakings. Of course, Germany was not the first country to violate treaties; nor was this by any means the first treaty Germany had violated; but there was an element of cynicism in the action with few parallels in modern Europe, and there was the virtual certainty that many more similar acts would soon be performed. The baleful precedent was indeed swiftly followed by others; and it required no high measure of prescience to perceive that in a very short time most other international undertakings would be similarly disregarded: not only by Germany but throughout the world. Even if Britain, France and Poland had all somehow contrived to avert involvement in war in 1939, some kind of Second World War was inevitable. It was also inevitable that the war would go on extending until the surviving states were prepared to observe a code of agreed behaviour towards one another. What ultimately emerged was perhaps little more than a common recognition of 'spheres of influence' belonging to the victors; a recognition founded more on fear of the alternative than on any high principles of behaviour. Be that as it may, it has sufficed for a third of a century to avert war between the major Powers. Better a 'balance of terror' than no balance at all. Perhaps people are no more moral than they were thirty-five or forty years ago; but they are more prudent to the extent that they now perceive more clearly the need to obey some kind of international order.

Notes

1 THE DIE IS CAST

1 Dalton diary, 11 April 1938.
2 The present author has described events of March 1938 to March 1939 in *In the Year of Munich* (Macmillan, 1977).
3 Memorandum on the situation after the absorption of Czecho-Slovakia . . . FO, 29 March 1939. CAB 21/754
4 Cabinet 12(39), 18 March. CAB 23/98.
5 Cabinet 13(39), 20 March. CAB 23/98.
6 FP (36) 36th meeting, 27 March 1939. CAB 27/624.
7 Cabinet 15(39), 29 March. CAB 23/98.
8 Idem.
9 Kennard to Halifax, 29 March 1939. DBFP 4 No. 564.
10 Neville to Hilda Chamberlain, 2 April 1939. NC 18/1/1092.
11 FP (36) 39th meeting, 30 March 1939. CAB 27/624.
12 Dalton diary, 30 March 1939. Dalton I/20.
13 FP (36) 40th meeting, 31 March 1939. CAB 27/624.
14 Runciman to Chamberlain, 31 March 1939(No. 2). NC 7/11/32/225.
15 Hankey to Phipps, 4 April 1939. PHPP 3/3, Fo. 99 seq.
16 Ogilvie-Forbes to Halifax, 5 April 1939. DBFP 5 No. 6.
17 Dalton diary, 21 June 1939.
18 Visit of Polish MFA, 4–6 April 1939. DBFP 5 No. 1.
19 Cabinet 18(39), 5 April. CAB 23/98.
20 On the latter point see Halifax to Phipps (draft), 28 September 1939. FO 371/23846, Fo. 93 seq.
21 Cabinets 18 and 19 of 1939, 5 and 10 April. CAB 23/98.
22 Cabinet 19(39), 10 April. CAB 23/98.
23 Neville to Hilda Chamberlain, 15 April 1939. NC 18/1/1094.
24 Cabinet 19(39), 10 April. CAB 23/98.
25 Idem.

2 REAPPRAISALS

1 Cabinet 16(39), 30 March. CAB 23/98.
2 Idem.
3 Cabinet 30(39), 24 May. Confidential annex (CA), CAB 23/99.
4 Cabinet 22(39), 24 April. CAB 23/99.
5 Neville to Ida Chamberlain, 26 March 1939. NC 18/1/1091.

6 Cabinet 21(39), 19 April. CAB 23/98.
7 CP 91(39). April 1939. CAB 24/285.
8 Ibid.
9 Cabinet 22(39), 24 April. CAB 23/99.
10 Neville to Hilda Chamberlain, 29 April 1939. NC 18/1/1096.
11 Dalton diary, 3 May 1939.

3 RUSSIA: STAGE ONE

1 FO minute, 3 January 1939. FO 371/23677, fo. 251 seq.
2 Cabinet 24(39), 26 April. CAB 23/98.
3 Orde (Riga) to Halifax, 15 April 1939. DBFP 5 No. 181.
4 FP (36), 50th meeting, 9 June 1939. CAB 27/625.
5 Governor-General of NZ, received 12 May 1939. Inskip memorandum, 22 May 1939. CAB 24/287.
6 Menzies to High Commissioner, received 22 May 1939. Idem.
7 C. T. te Water, *aide-mémoires*, 22 April 1939, 19 May 1939. Idem.
8 UK High Commissioner in Canada, telegram, 27 April 1939. Idem.
9 Telegram B 157 to Dominions, 15 April 1939. CAB 21/551.
10 Halifax to Seeds, 14 April 1939. DBFP 5 No. 170.
11 Seeds to Halifax, 18 April 1939. DBFP 5 No. 201.
12 Kennard to Halifax, 18 April 1939. DBFP 5 No. 204.
13 FO comments on Russian proposals: Appendix II to FP (36), 43rd meeting, 19 April 1939. CAB 27/624.
14 Military value of Russia, CP 95(39), 24 April 1939. CAB 24/285.
15 FP (36), 44th meeting, 25 April 1939. CAB 27/624.
16 Military value of Russia, CP 95(39) 25 April. CAB 24/285.
17 FP (36), 44th meeting, 25 April 1939. CAB 27/624.
18 C.P. 95(39), supra.
19 FP (36), 44th meeting, 25 April 1939. CAB 27/624.
20 FP (36), 43rd meeting, 19 April 1939. CAB 27/624.
21 Phipps to Halifax, 3 May 1939. DBFP 5 No. 351.
22 Seeds to Halifax, 4 May 1939. DBFP 5 No. 353.
23 Henderson to Halifax, 5 May 1939. DBFP 5 No. 383.
24 Henderson to Halifax, 5 May 1939. DBFP 5 No. 383.
25 Loraine to Halifax, 8 May 1939. DBFP 5 No. 409.
26 Seeds to Halifax, 9 May 1939. DBFP 5 No. 421. See *Parl. Deb.* 5.s HC, Vol. 346, cols 131–40.
27 Seeds to Halifax, 15 May 1939. DBFP 5 No. 520.
28 Phipps to Halifax, 17 May 1939. CAB 21/551.
29 Negotiations with Soviet Russia...(c. 16 May 1939). CAB 27/625.
30 Vansittart memorandum, ?15 May 1939. CAB 27/625.
31 Neville to Ida Chamberlain, 21 May 1939. NC 18/1/1100.
32 Cabinet 30(39), 24 May. CAB 23/99.
33 UK Delegation (Geneva) to Cadogan, 22 May 1939. DBFP 5 Nos 581–2.
34 Neville to Hilda Chamberlain, 28 May 1939. NC 18/1/1101.
35 Halifax to Seeds, 24 May 1939. DBFP 5 No. 609.
36 UK Delegation (Geneva) to Halifax, 25 May 1939. DBFP 5 No. 621.

4 RUSSIA: STAGE TWO

1 Seeds to Halifax 27 May 1939. DBFP 5 No. 645.
2 FP (36), 49th meeting, 5 June 1939. CAB 27/625.
3 Cabinet 32(39), 14 June. CAB 23/99.
4 FP (36), 50th meeting, 9 June 1939, CAB 27/625.
5 Neville to Ida Chamberlain, 10 June 1939. NC 18/1/1102.
6 FP (36), 53rd meeting, 20 June 1939. CAB 27/625.
7 Cabinet 33(39), 21 June. CAB 23/100.
8 FP (36), 53rd meeting, 20 June 1939. CAB 27/625.
9 FP (36), 54th meeting, 26 June 1939. CAB 27/625.
10 FP (36), 50th meeting, 9 June 1939. CAB 27/625.
11 FP (36), 54th meeting, 26 June 1939. CAB 27/625.
12 Cabinet 34(39), 28 June. CAB 23/100.
13 Cabinet 35(39), 5 July. CAB 23/100.
14 Dalton diary, 29 June 1939 (views of Raczynski).
15 FP (36), 56th meeting, 4 July 1939. CAB 27/625.
16 Cabinet 35(39), 5 July. CAB 23/100.
17 Cabinet 37(39), 12 July. CAB 23/100.
18 FP (36), 58th meeting, 19 July 1939. CAB 27/625.
19 Cabinet 38(39), 19 July. CAB 23/100.
20 FP (36), 58th meeting, 19 July 1939. CAB 27/625.
21 Bonnet to Halifax, 19 July 1939. DBFP 6 No. 358.
22 Neville to Ida Chamberlain, 23 July 1939. NC 18/1/1108.
23 Halifax to Seeds, 21 July 1939. DBFP 6 No. 378.
24 Cabinet 39(39), 26 July. CAB 23/100.
25 Cabinet 40(39), 2 August. CAB 23/100.
26 Dalton diary, 16 August 1939.
27 Cabinet 41(39), 22 August. CAB 23/100.
28 Dalton diary, 22 August 1939.
29 Cabinet 41(39), 22 August CAB 23/100.
30 Idem.
31 Dalton diary, 22 August 1939.
32 UK Delegation (Geneva) to Cadogan, 22 May 1939. DBFP 5 No. 581.
33 Cabinet 30(39), 24 May. CAB 23/100.
34 Meeting with NCL delegation, 28 June 1939. PREM 1/325.
35 Dalton diary, 13 February 1940.
36 Cabinet 26(39), 3 May. CAB 23/99.
37 Henderson to Halifax, 8 June 1939. FO 800/315, fo. 165 seq.
38 FP (36), 54th meeting, 26 June 1939. CAB 27/625.
39 Implications of the situation in Europe and the Far East, 27 August 1939. CAB 21/754.

5 HOPES FORLORN

1 Henderson to Halifax, 11 June 1939 (copy). PREM 1/331A.
2 Halifax to Chamberlain, 19 August 1939. PREM 1/331A.
3 Idem.

4 Chamberlain to Hitler, 22 August 1939 (copy). PREM 1/331.
5 Inskip diary, 23 August 1939. INKP 2.
6 Hankey diary, 23 August 1939. HNKY 1/7.
7 Memorandum, not signed, 18 August 1939. FO 371/23130, fo. 291 seq.
8 Hankey diary, 25 August 1939. HNKY 1/7.
9 Henderson to Halifax, 25 August 1939. PREM 1/331A.
10 Cabinet 43(39), 26 August. CAB 23/100.
11 Cabinet 44(39), 27 August. CAB 23/100.
12 Crown Prince of Sweden to Chamberlain, 31 May 1939. PREM 1/328.
13 Various papers, June–July 1939. PREM 1/328.
14 Dahlerus record (covered by Cadogan to Halifax, 16 April 1943), Hickelton A.4.410.3.10(i).
15 Note, not addressed, but stamped '(Signed) Halifax', 29 July 1939. FO 800/316, fo. 134 seq.
16 Cabinet 44(39), 27 August. CAB 23/100.
17 Idem.
18 Henderson telegram No. 499, 12.30 a.m., 30 August 1939. PREM 1/331A.
19 Henderson telegram (by telephone), 29 August. Idem.
20 Idem.
21 Wilson note for Chamberlain, 30 August 1939. Idem.
22 Cabinet 46(39), 30 August. CAB 23/100.
23 Cabinet 46(39), 30 August. CAB 23/100; Halifax to Henderson, 30 August 1939. DBFP 7 No. 543.
24 Kennard to Halifax, 31 August 1939, 6.30 p.m. PREM 1/331A.
25 Inskip diary, 31 August 1939. INKP 2.
26 Idem.
27 Cabinet 47(39), 1 September. CAB 23/100.
28 Idem.
29 Inskip diary, 1 September 1939. INKP 2.
30 Halifax to Phipps, 2 (misnumbered 1) September 1939, 11.50 a.m. DBFP 7 No. 699.
31 Phipps to Halifax, 2 September 1939, 1.30 p.m. PREM 1/331A, fo. 62; DBFP 7 No. 708.
32 Halifax to Chamberlain, 14 August 1939. PREM 1/331A.
33 Henderson to Halifax, 25 August 1939. FO 800/316, fo. 227 seq.; but contracts Raczynski's view in Dalton diary, 22 August 1939. Dalton I/22.
34 Loraine to Halifax, 23 August 1939. CAB 23/100: annex to minutes of 24 August.
35 A record of events before the war 1939 (Halifax) No. FO 800/317, fo. 82 seq.
36 Loraine to Halifax, 1 September 1939. DBFP 7 No. 653.
37 Memorandum, n.d., n.s., PREM 1/351A, fos 59–60, identified in DBFP 7 as Minute to Harvey, 2 September, quoted in Cabinet 48(39).
38 Idem.
39 Cabinet 48(39), 2 September 1939, 4.15 p.m. CAB 23/100.
40 Halifax: A record of events . . . N.D. FO 800/317, fo. 82 seq.
41 Cabinet 48(39), 2 September, 4.15 p.m. CAB 23/100.
42 Halifax: A record of events. N.O. FO 800/317, fo. 82 seq.
43 Neville to Ida Chamberlain, 10 September 1939. NC 18/1/1116.
44 Inskip diary 2, 3 September. INKP 2.

45 Cabinet 49(39), 2 September, 11.30 p.m. CAB 23/100.
46 Cabinet 49(39), 2 September, 11.30 p.m. CAB 23/100.
47 Halifax, Record of events . . . N.D. FO 800/317, fo. 82 seq.

6 ADJUSTMENT TO WAR

1 Hankey diary, 23 August 1939. HNKY 1/7.
2 Memorandum, 'A War Cabinet' for Sir Horace Wilson, 24 August 1939. HNKY 10/1, fo. 2, 3.
3 Hankey diary, 23 August 1939. HNKY 1/7.
4 Idem.
5 Churchill to Chamberlain, 2 September 1939. NC 7/9/45.
6 Dalton diary, 24 August 1939. Dalton I/21.
7 Idem, 25 August.
8 NEC/PEC joint meeting, 2 September 1939. LPEC vol. 80, fo. 611.
9 Churchill to Chamberlain, 2 September 1939. NC 7/9/45.
10 Dalton diary, 6 September 1939.
11 Sinclair memoranda.
12 Sinclair memoranda.
13 Idem.
14 Inskip diary, 2 September 1939. INKP 2.
15 Sinclair memoranda.
16 Cadogan to Phipps, 6 September 1939. PHPP 2/1, fos 32–3.
17 Cadogan to Phipps, 27 September, 7 October 1939. PHPP 2/1, fos 34–6.
18 War Cabinet minutes 3 (WM 3(39)); WM 6.5, 6 September. CAB 65/1.
19 Dulanty to Chamberlain, 31 August 1939 (message) PREM 1/341; Rucker to Hankinson, 5 September 1939 (copy). Idem.
20 WM 2(39), 4 September. CAB 65/1.
21 WM 5(39), 5 September. CAB 65/1.
22 Neville to Ida Chamberlain, 10 September 1939. NC 18/1/1116.
23 Neville to Hilda Chamberlain, 17 September 1939. NC 18/1/1121.
24 WM 18(39), 17 September. CAB 65/1.
25 Dalton diary, 18 September 1939.
26 Seeds to Halifax, 13 September 1939. FO 371/23135, fo. 40.
27 WM 18(39), 17 September. CAB 65/1.
28 WM 28(39), 26 September. CA, CAB 65/3.
29 Orde to Halifax, 18 September 1939. FO 371/23609, fo. 209
30 Halifax to Seeds, 27 September 1939. FO 371/23697, fo. 173 seq.
31 Preston to Halifax, 2 October 1939. FO 371/23135, fo. 52.
32 Leipu to Cadogan, 26 September 1939. FO 371/23135, fo. 44 seq.
33 Dalton diary, 11 September 1939.
34 Dalton diary, 3 October 1939 (views of Sir Kingsley Wood).
35 Noel report to Daladier (translation). 15 October 1939. FO 371/23149, fo. 96 seq.
36 Dalton diary, 13 September 1939.
37 WM 2(39), 4 September. CAB 65/1.
38 WM 4(39), 5 September, CA, CAB 65/3.
39 WM 4(39), 13 September. CAB 65/1.

40 Robin Hankey to Hankey, 12 September 1939 (copy). HNKY 10/1, fo. 7.
41 WM 16(39), 15 September 1939. CA, CAB 65/3.
42 Churchill to Chamberlain, 15 September 1939. NC 7/9/49.
43 WM 35(39), 3 October. CAB 65/1.
44 WM 31(39), 29 September. CAB 65/1.
45 WM 9(39), 9 September. CAB 65/1.
46 Neville to Ida Chamberlain, 22 September 1939. NC 18/1/1122.
47 WM 49(39), 16 October. CAB 65/1.
48 Dalton diary, 18 October 1939. Dalton I/21.
49 WM 49(39), 16 October. CAB 65/1.
50 351 *Parl. Deb.* 5.s, 3 September 1939, col. 301.
51 *Daily Worker*, 23 November 1939.
52 Dalton diary, 16 December 1939. Dalton I/21.
53 Neville to Ida Chamberlain, 22 September 1939. NC 18/1/1122.
54 Neville to Ida Chamberlain, 8 October 1939. NC 18/1/1124.
55 Hankey to Halifax, 12 September 1939. FO 800/317, fos 7–8.
56 Hankey to Halifax, 27 September 1939. FO 800/317, fo. 53 seq.
57 351 *Parl. Deb.* 5.s, col. 299, 3 September 1939.
58 Chamberlain to Lloyd George, 4 September 1939. LG G/4/2/3.
59 WM 12(39), 11 September. CAB 65/1; Churchill/Lloyd George correspondence, 12, 13 September 1939. LG G/4/5/37, 38.
60 WM 30(39), 28 September. CAB 65/1.
61 351 *Parl. Deb.* 5.s., col. 1871, 3 October 1939.
62 Lloyd George to Liddell Hart, 20 November 1939 (copy). LG G/9/3/3.
63 WM 34(39) and 38(39), 2, 5 October 1939. CA, CAB 65/3.
64 Hankey memorandum, 29 September 1939. HNKY 10/3, fos 1–4.
65 WM 31(39), 29 September. CAB 65/1.
66 Neville to Ida Chamberlain, 8 October 1939. NC 18/1/1124.
67 WM 47(39), 14 October. CAB 65/1.
68 Neville to Hilda Chamberlain, 12 November 1939. NC 18/1/1131.
69 Halifax to Lytton, 11 November 1939(copy). FO 800/317, fo. 196 seq.
70 Brocket to Halifax, 9 November 1939. FO 800/317, fo. 193 seq.
71 Memorandum on Peace Aims, 10 November 1939. PREM 1/380.
72 Neville to Ida Chamberlain, 3 December 1939. NC 18/1/1133A.

7 NORTHERN LIGHTS

1 Sir R. Hoare to Halifax, 30 September 1939. FO 371/23678, fo. 93.
2 Vansittart minute, 2 October 1939. FO 371/23678, fo. 92.
3 Seeds to Halifax, 12 October 1939. FO 371/23678, fo. 182 seq.
4 Sir R. Hoare to Halifax, 27 September 1939. FO 371/23846, fo. 79.
5 Sargent memorandum, 26 September 1939. FO 371/23846, fos 88–9.
6 Halifax to Phipps, 28 September 1939. FO 371/23846, fo. 93 seq.
7 Gallienne to Halifax, 29 September 1939. FO 371/23689, fo. 33.
8 Seeds to Halifax, 6 October 1939. FO 371/23689, fo. 78 seq.
9 Seeds to Halifax, 11 October 1939. FO 371/23689, fo. 121.
10 Gallienne reports, 7, 9 October 1939. FO 371/23610; *The Times*, 9 October 1939.

11 *The Times*, (?)20 October 1939. FO 371/23697, fo. 250.
12 T. Preston(Kovno) report, 22 May 1939. FO 371/23601.
13 Preston report, 5 September 1939. FO 371/23609.
14 Seeds to Halifax, 11 October 1939. FO 371/23692, fo. 106.
15 Preston to Halifax, 11 October, 17 October, 19 October 1939. FO 371/23689, fos 147, 244, 269 seq.
16 Vale report, 8 November 1939. FO 371/23610.
17 Preston to Orde, 4 November 1939(copy). FO 371/23610.
18 Resumé of Russo-Finnish negotiations, October 12 – November 13 1939. FO 371/23693, fo. 163 seq.
19 Idem.
20 Halifax to Seeds, 16 October 1939 (draft). FO 371/23697, fo. 261 seq.
21 WM 57(39), 23 October. CAB 65/1.
22 WM 57(39); the telegram is set out in WP (39)109, CAB 66/3.
23 WM 67(39), 1 November. CAB 65/2.
24 WM 67(39); WP (39)107.
25 WM 69(39), 3 November. CAB 65/2.
26 Seeds to Halifax, 15, 16 November 1939. FO 371/23678, fos 193, 197.
27 Elliot memorandum, 20 November 1939, FO 371/23678, fo. 220.
28 Seeds to Halifax, 24 November 1939. FO 371/23678, fo. 240.
29 Laurence Collier memorandum for Sargent, 1 December 1939. FO 371/23693, fo. 240 seq.
30 WM 103(39), 4 December. CAB 65/2.
31 WM 116(39), 15 December. CAB 65/2.
32 Orde to Halifax, 13 December 1939. FO 371/23698, fo. 112 seq.
33 Neville to Ida Chamberlain, 3 December 1939. NC 18/1/1133A.
34 Loraine to Halifax, 5 December 1939. FO 371/23695, fo. 146.
35 Snow to Halifax, 10 December 1939. FO 371/23695, fo. 90.
36 Clark-Kerr (Shanghai) to Halifax, 11 December 1939. FO 371/23695, fo. 198.
37 Halifax note for Butler, 7 December 1939. FO 371/23694, fo. 203.
38 Draft minutes of meeting . . . 9 January 1940. PREM 1/419.
39 WM 122(39), 22 December. CA, CAB 65/4.
40 Churchill to Chamberlain, 25 December 1939. NC 7/9/69.
41 WM 1(40), 2 January. CA, CAB 65/11.
42 WM 122(39), 22 December. CA, CAB 65/4.
43 Monson to Halifax, 22 December 1939. FO 371/24860, fos, 417 seq.
44 WM 123(39), 27 December. CA, CAB 65/4.
45 WM 1(40), 2(40), 1, 2 January. CA, CAB 65/11; also WP (39)179; WP (39)180.
46 WM 4(40), 5 January. CA, CAB 65/11.
47 WM 5(40), 6 January. CA, CAB 65/11.
48 WM 7(40), 8 January. CA, CAB 65/11.
49 Idem.
50 Draft minutes of meeting . . . 9 January 1940. PREM 1/419.
51 Eden to Chamberlain, 10 January 1940. PREM 1/419.
52 Menzies/Smuts cables 12 January 1940. PREM 1/419.
53 WM 10(40), 12 January. CA, CAB 65/11.
54 Chief of Naval Staff reporting COS view, WM 18(40), 19 January. CA, CAB 65/11.

55 WM 18(40), 19 January. CA, CAB 65/11.
56 WM 18(40), 22 January. CA, CAB 65/11.
57 Idem.
58 Idem.
59 Eden to Chamberlain, 2 February 1940. PREM 1/437.
60 WM 35(40), 7 February. CA, CAB 65/11.
61 WM 35(40), 7 February. CAB 65/5.
62 Halifax to Chamberlain, 10 February 1940. PREM 1/408.
63 WM (40)39, 12 February. CAB 65/11.
64 WM (40)44, 17 February. CAB 65/11.
65 WM (40)45, 18 February. CA, CAB 65/11.
66 Chamberlain to Daladier, 15 February 1940 (copy). PREM 1/408.
67 Instructions to Brigadier Ling, 18 February 1940. WM (40)45, CA, CAB 65/11.
68 WM (40)46, 19 February. CA, CAB 65/11.

8 FROM ONE WAR TO ANOTHER

1 WM 44(40), 17 February. CAB 65/5.
2 WM 46(40), 19 February. CA, CAB 65/11.
3 See WP (40)60.
4 WM 46(40), 19 February. CA, CAB 65/11.
5 Cambon memorandum, 22 February 1940 (translation). FO 371/24846, fo. 109 seq.; WM (40)52, 26 February. CA, CAB 65/11.
6 Cambon memorandum, 22 February 1940 (translation). FO 371/24846, fo. 109.
7 WM 53(40), 27 February 1940. CA, CAB 65/11.
8 WM 57(40), 1 March. CA, CAB 65/12.
9 WM 56(40), 1 March (1). CAB 65/12.
10 WM 57(40), 1 March (2). CA, CAB 65/12.
11 Idem.
12 Idem.
13 WM 63(40), 8 March. CA, CAB 65/12.
14 WM 61(40), 6 March. CA, CAB 65/12.
15 Idem.
16 WM 60(40), 5 March. CA, CAB 65/12.
17 WM 62(40), 7 March. CA, CAB 65/12.
18 Idem.
19 Idem.
20 WM 64(40), 9 March. CA, CAB 65/12.
21 Idem.
22 WM 66(40), 12 March. CA, CAB 65/12.
23 Vereker to Halifax, 13 March 1940. FO 371/24794, fo. 137 seq.
24 Le Rougetel (Moscow) to Halifax, 16 March 1940. FO 371/24794, fos 212-3.
25 Vereker to Halifax, 13 March 1940). *loc. cit.*
26 Vereker to Halifax, 14 March 1940. FO 371/24794, fo. 160.
27 WM 68(40), 14 March. CAB 65/6.
28 WM 69(40), 15 March. CAB 65/6.

29 Stanley, reporting British Military Attaché. Idem.
30 WM 69(40), 71(40), 15, 18 March. CAB 65/6.
31 WM 68(40), 14 March 1940. CA, CAB 65/12.
32 Ibid.
33 Ibid.
34 WM 70(40), 16 March. CAB 65/6; for fuller record see Halifax to Campbell, 15 March 1940. FO 371/24824, fo. 256 seq.
35 WM 72(40), 19 March. CAB 65/6.
36 WP (40)91 (= COS (40)252), 8 March 1940. FO 371/24846, fo. 100 seq.
37 Dalton diary, 23 February 1940. Dalton I/22.
38 Chatfield to Halifax, 27 March 1940. FO 371/24846, fo. 201 seq.
39 See, e.g., Halifax to Cadogan, 25 March 1940. FO 371/24846, fo. 167.
40 See, e.g., WP (40), 84. March 1940. CAB 66/6, fo. 71 seq.
41 WM 74(40), 21 March. CAB 65/6.
42 WM 73(40), 20 March. CAB 65/6.
43 Policy to be adopted . . . 26 March 1940. WP (40)107. CAB 66/6.
44 WM 77(40), 29 March. CAB 65/6.
45 WM 77(40), 29 March. CA, CAB 65/12.
46 UK High Commissioner telegram, 31 March 1940. FO 371/24846 fo. 224.
47 WM 78(40), 1 April. CAB 65/6.
48 Note by Chamberlain, 31 March 1940. PREM 1/419.
49 WM 84(40), 8 April. CA, CAB 65/12.
50 Stevenson memorandum for Halifax, 4 April 1940. PREM 1/419; Chamberlain draft of letter to Daladier. Idem.
51 Idem.
52 WM 80(40), 3 April. CA, CAB 65/12.
53 Churchill to Chamberlain, 6 April 1940. PREM 1/419.
54 WM 82(40), 5 April. CAB 65/6.
55 Telegrams to Dormer, Mallet, 4 April 1940 (copies). FO 371/24815, fo. 391 seq.; see also WP (40)107, 26 March 1940. CAB 66/6.
56 Ibid.
57 WM 83(40), 6 April. CAB 65/6.
58 Dormer to Halifax, 5 April 1940. FO 371/24815, fo. 424.
59 Mallet to Cadogan, 7 April 1940 (copy). FO 371/24815, fo. 121 seq.

9 THINGS FALL APART . . .

1 Neville to Hilda Chamberlain, 6 April 1940. NC 18/1/1149.
2 Smith (Copenhagen), 5 (despatched 6) April 1939. FO 371/24815, fo. 429.
3 To C-in-C Home Fleet, 7 April 1940. FO 371/24815, fo. 58.
4 Campbell to Halifax, 11 April 1940. FO 371/24815, fo. 53 seq.
5 WM 87(40), 10 April. CAB 65/6.
6 Plan R4 . . . WP (40)122. CAB 66/7.
7 WM 87(40), 10 April. CAB 65/6.
8 Idem.
9 WM 87(40), 10 April. CA, CAB 65/12.
10 WM 88(40), 11 April. CAB 65/12.
11 WM 89(40), 12 April. CA, CAB 65/12.

12 Mallet (Evans for Churchill), 13 April 1940. FO 371/24834, fo. 201.
13 Neville to Hilda Chamberlain, 4 May 1940. NC 18/1/1153.
14 Campbell to Halifax, 13 April 1940. FO 371/24834, fo. 209.
15 WM 92(40), 14 April. CA, CAB 65/12; WM 97(40), 19 April. CAB 65/6.
16 WM 98(40), 16 April. CA, CAB 65/12.
17 WM 98(40), 20 April. CA, CAB 65/12.
18 Idem. See also WP (40)133, 20 April. CAB 66/7.
19 WM 99(40), 21 April. CA, CAB 65/12.
20 Idem.
21 WM 100(40), 22 April. CA, CAB 65/12.
22 WM 98(40), 20 April. CA, CAB 65/12.
23 WM 99(40), 21 April. CA, CAB 65/12.
24 WM 102(40), 24 April. CAB 65/6.
25 WM 104(40), 26 April. CAB 65/6.
26 Idem.
27 Ibid.
28 WM 104(40), 26 April. CA, CAB 65/12.
29 WM 105(40), 27 April. CAB 65/12.
30 Idem.
31 Neville to Ida Chamberlain, 27 April 1940. NC 18/1/1152. Reynaud to Chamberlain, 26 April 1940 (copy). PREM 1/419.
32 WM 109-112(40), 1-4 May. CAB 65/7.
33 WM 100(40), 22 April. CA, CAB 65/12.
34 WM 101-106(40), 23-8 April. CAB 65/6.
35 WM 106(40), 28 April. CAB 65/6.
36 WP (40)144, quoted in WM 113(40), 6 May. CA, CAB 65/13.
37 WM 112(40), 4 May. CAB 65/7.
38 WM 105(40), 27 April. CAB 65/6.
39 WM 112(40), 4 May. CAB 65/7.
40 WM 113(40), 6 May. CA, CAB 65/13.
41 WM 88(40), 11 April. CAB 65/6.
42 WM 89(40), 12 April. CAB 65/6.
43 Legation Report No. 17, 9 May 1940. FO 371/24859, fo. 116 seq.
44 WM 88(40), 11 April. CAB 65/6.
45 Notes of informal meeting...Thursday 11 April 1940. FO 371/24834, fo. 242 seq.
46 Legation Report No. 17., 9 May 1940. FO 371/24859, fo. 116 seq.
47 WM 95(40), 17 April. CAB 65/6.
48 WM 91(40), 13 April. CA, CAB 65/12.
49 Hankey to Halifax, 24 April 1940. FO 800/322, fo. 258 seq.
50 WM 103(40), 25 April. CA, CAB 65/12.
51 WM 109(40), 1 May. CAB 65/7.
52 Postal censorship report...1 June 1940. FO 371/24859, fo. 147 seq.
53 WM 87(40), 10 April. CAB 65/6.
54 WM 92(40), 14 April. CAB 65/6.
55 WM 115(40), 8 May. CAB 65/7.
56 See, e.g., Craigie to Halifax, 11 April 1940. FO 24815, fo. 84; WM 95(40), 17 April. CAB 65/6.
57 Campbell to Halifax, 2 April 1940. FO 371/24846, fo. 232.

58 See, e.g., Corbin note, 5 April 1940. FO 371/24846, fo. 248 seq.
59 SWC resolution, 23 April 1940. WP (40)135, CAB 66/5.
60 Dominions circular telegram, 20 April 1940. FO 371/24846, fo. 212.
61 Le Rougetel to Halifax, 10 April 1940. FO 371/24815, fo. 61.
62 Meeting of Ministers, 11 April 1940. FO 800/321, fo. 86.
63 WM 92(40), 15 April. CAB 65/6.
64 WM 77(40), 29 March. CAB 65/6.
65 Idem.
66 WM 106(40), 30 Arpil. CAB 65/6.
67 WM 113(40), 6 May. CAB 65/7.
68 Halifax to Wedgwood, 16 April 1940 (copy). FO 24847, fos 42–3.
69 WM 88(40), 11 April. CAB 65/6.
70 WM 89(40), 12 April. CAB 65/6.
71 WM 92(40), 14 April. CAB 65/6.
72 WM 94(40), 16 April. CAB 65/6.
73 Osborne/Nichols correspondence 26 April, 6 May 1940. FO 371/24943, fos 172–3; 174.
74 WM 105(40), 27 April. CAB 65/6.
75 Vansittart note for Halifax, 19 April 1940. FO 371/24942, fos 290–1.
76 WP (40)134, 21 April. CAB 66/7.
77 Loraine to Halifax, 4 May 1940 (copy). FO 371/24943, fo. 344 seq.
78 WM 107(40), 29 April. CAB 65/6.
79 The Balkan front, WP (40)139, 29 April 1940. CAB 66/7.
80 Review of the strategical situation . . .WP (40)145, 4 May. CAB 66/7.
81 WM 87(40), 10 April. CAB 65/6.
82 WM 90(40), 12 April. CA, CAB 65/12.
83 SWC resolutions, 23 April 1940. WP (40)135. CAB 66/7,
84 WM 109(40), 1 May. CAB 65/7.
85 WM 109(40), 1 May. CA, CAB 65/13.
86 WM 109(40), 1 May. CAB 65/7.
87 WM 110(40), 2 May. CAB 65/7.
88 WM 114(40), 7 May. CAB 65/7.

10 POLITICAL CRISIS

1 See Labour Party leaflet, *c.* October 1939. LPEC 80, fo. 706, etc.
2 Attlee to Middleton, 25 January 1940 (copy). Attlee Box 8.
3 Dalton diary, 6 September 1939.
4 Dalton diary, middle of February 1940.
5 Dalton diary, 17 March 1940.
6 Neville to Ida Chamberlain, 7 January 1940. NC 18/1/1137.
7 Neville to Hilda Chamberlain, 20 April 1940. NC 18/1/1151.
8 Idem.
9 Churchill to Chamberlain, 24 April 1940 (copy). NC 7/9/78.
10 Neville to Ida Chamberlain, 27 April 1940. NC 18/1/1152.
11 Neville to Hilda Chamberlain, 4 May 1940. NC 18/1/1153.
12 Neville to Ida Chamberlain, 27 April 1940. NC 18/1/1152.
13 WM 106(40), 28 April. CA, CAB 65/12.

14　WM 112(40), 4 May. CAB 65/7.
15　Idem.
16　See Dalton diary, 4, 5 May 1940.
17　Keyes to Churchill, 30 March 1940 (copy). FO 800/322, fo. 261 seq.
18　*News Chronicle*, 1 May 1940.
19　*Daily Mirror*, 2 May 1940.
20　*Daily Herald*, 3 May 1940 (political correspondent).
21　*Daily Telegraph*, 6 May 1940.
22　*The Times*, 6 May 1940.
23　*Daily Express*, 7 May 1940.
24　Dalton diary, 8 May 1940. Dalton I/22.
25　Idem.
26　Dalton diary, 8 May 1940.
27　Dalton diary, 9 May 1940.
28　*The Times*, 10 May 1940.
29　Newspapers of 9 May 1940.
30　Rothermere to Chamberlain 7 May 1940 (telegram). NC 7/11/33/144.
31　Menzies to Chamberlain, 11 May 1940 (telegram). NC 7/11/33/12.
32　Dalton diary, 8 May 1940.
33　Butler to Halifax, 9 May 1940. Hickleton A4.410.16.
34　See, e.g., Dalton diary, 2 May 1940.
35　Dalton diary, 9 May 1940.
36　*Daily Mail*, 9 May 1940.
37　Dalton diary, 10 May 1940.
38　Minutes of NEC, 10 May 1940. LPEC vol. 82, fo. 313.
39　WM 119(40), 10 May, 4.30 p.m. CAB 65/7.
40　Neville to Ida Chamberlain, 11 May 1940. NC 18/1/1155.
41　Neville to Ida Chamberlain, 11 May 1940. NC 18/1/1155.
42　*Daily Worker*, 15 May 1940.
43　'Candidus', *Daily Sketch*, 9 May 1940.
44　Chamberlain to Churchill, 11 May 1940 (copy). NC 7/9/82.
45　Dalton diary, 11 May 1940.

11　RETROSPECT

1　Monson to Halifax, 22 December 1939. FO 371/24860, fo. 417 seq.
2　Monson to Halifax, 12 October 1939. FO 371/23697, fo. 251 seq.
3　Notes by FSL . . . 5 January 1937. CHT/3/1, fo. 193 seq.
4　Chamberlain to Arnold, 10 January 1940 (copy). NC 7/11/33/6.

Abbreviations and Bibliographical Note

The main primary sources used, and the abbreviations used in footnotes to the text, may be conveniently indicated together. As the object of the book has been to retell the story of events from the period 1939–40 so far as possible from primary sources, an extensive bibliography of secondary sources would be inappropriate.

ATTLEE: Clement (Earl) Attlee papers, University College, Oxford.

CAB: Cabinet papers, Public Record Office, Kew, Surrey.

CHT: Lord Chatfield papers, Royal Maritime Museum, Greenwich, London. S.E.3.

DALTON DIARY Hugh (Lord) Dalton papers, British Library of Political and Economic Science, London School of Economics, London W.C.2.

DBFP: Documents on British Foreign Policy, 3rd. Series. HMSO.

FO: Foreign Office papers, Public Record Office, Kew, Surrey.

HICKLETON: Hickleton papers (Viscount, later Earl, Halifax). Churchill College, Cambridge.

HNKY: Lord Hankey papers, Churchill College, Cambridge.

INKP: Sir Thomas Inskip (Viscount Caldecote) papers, Churchill College, Cambridge.

L.G.: David Lloyd George (Earl Lloyd-George) papers, Beaverbrook Library. Now at House of Lords Record Office, London. S.W.1.

LPEC: Labour Party Executive Committee Minutes, Transport House, Smith Square, London S.W.1.

PHPP: Sir Eric Phipps papers, Churchill College,
                 Cambridge.
PREM: Premier papers, Public Record Office, Kew,
                 Surrey.
SINCLAIR   Sir Archibald Sinclair (Viscount Thurso) notes,
MEMORANDA: National Liberal Club, London S.W.1.
U.R.O.   Ulster Record Office, Belfast.
W.M.:   War Cabinet Minutes, See CAB.

The main Newspapers used were:
  Daily Herald
  Daily Mail
  Daily Mirror
  Daily Sketch
  Daily Telegraph
  Daily Worker
  Evening News
  News Chronicle
  The Times.

The other main printed sources were: Hansard (*Parl. Deb.* 5.s);
Documents on British Foreign Policy (Third Series) (DBFP); Sir
Llewellyn Woodward: *British Foreign Policy in the Second World War*
(London: HMSO, 1970), vol. 1.

Index